Supporting Life Skills for Y with Vision Impairment an Disabilities

This practical resource is designed to help professionals, parents and carers as they support children with vision impairments to develop independence in everyday tasks. Using the Early Years Foundation Stage framework as a basis, it provides a wealth of strategies and activities to develop key skills, including dressing, maintaining personal hygiene, eating and drinking and road safety.

This is an invaluable tool that can be dipped in and out of to help make learning fun, boosting the child's confidence and helping create a positive 'can-do' attitude when faced with new challenges.

This book:

◆ Addresses the main problem areas for babies and young visually impaired children and their families, by providing simple explanations of skills and offering strategies and techniques to support progression onto the next stage.

◆ Is written in a fully accessible style, with photocopiable pages and additional downloadable resources.

◆ Provides a variety of documentation to chart the child's development and show progress over time.

Research shows strong indicators that early intervention can reduce or eliminate developmental delays in children with a vision impairment. The supporting strategies in this book help busy professionals and carers to make every opportunity a learning opportunity, allowing children with a vision impairment to become confident and independent individuals.

Fiona Broadley has worked for the last 30 years, exclusively teaching mobility and independent living skills to children and young people with vision impairments, many of whom have additional needs.

As the Chair of Habilitation VIUK (formerly MISE), she assisted in the gathering of research for the Mobility21 Project, which ultimately led to the creation of the National Quality Standards for the delivery of habilitation training and the creation of the new profession of habilitation specialist.

She heads a team of registered qualified habilitation specialists, all of whom have contributed to the ideas and practice found within this book. She now also lectures to student habilitation specialists at Birmingham City University, and with her team delivers the habilitation elements of the training for specialist teachers of the visually impaired at the University of Birmingham.

She lives in (not so) rural Warwickshire with her family and the school buddy dog, Griff.

Supporting Life Skills for Young Children with Vision Impairment and Other Disabilities

An Early Years Habilitation Handbook

Fiona Broadley

Routledge
Taylor & Francis Group

LONDON AND NEW YORK

First published 2021
by Routledge
2 Park Square, Milton Park, Abingdon, Oxon OX14 4RN

and by Routledge
52 Vanderbilt Avenue, New York, NY 10017

Routledge is an imprint of the Taylor & Francis Group, an informa business

British Library Cataloguing-in-Publication Data
A catalogue record for this book is available from the British Library

Library of Congress Cataloging-in-Publication Data
Names: Broadley, Fiona, author.
Title: Supporting life skills for young children with vision impairment and other disabilities : an early years habilitation handbook / Fiona Broadley.
Description: Abingdon, Oxon; New York, NY: Routledge, 2020. |
Includes bibliographical references.
Identifiers: LCCN 2020010569 (print) | LCCN 2020010570 (ebook) |
ISBN 9780367513122 (hardback) | ISBN 9780367435783 (paperback) |
ISBN 9781003004448 (ebook)
Subjects: LCSH: Children with visual disabilities. |
Children with visual disabilities–Great Britain. | Child development. |
Life skills. Classification: LCC HV1596.2 .B76 2020 (print) |
LCC HV1596.2 (ebook) | DDC 649/.6087–dc23
LC record available at https://lccn.loc.gov/2020010569
LC ebook record available at https://lccn.loc.gov/2020010570

ISBN: 978-0-367-51312-2 (hbk)
ISBN: 978-0-367-43578-3 (pbk)
ISBN: 978-1-003-00444-8 (ebk)

Typeset in Avant Garde
by Newgen Publishing UK

Visit the eResource: www.routledge.com/9780367435783

Printed and bound by CPI Group (UK) Ltd, Croydon CR0 4YY

Contents

Contents

Common terms used in this book

◆ **You** will refer to the parent, guardian, carer or professional supporting the child.

◆ The use of **he, she** or **they** is interchangeable when referring to the child.

◆ The book will use the term **vision impairment** to refer to a range of different eye conditions affecting vision. A child may be referred to as **vision impaired** or **severely vision impaired**, which may be abbreviated to **VI** or **SVI** respectively. Occasionally, the terms **sight impaired** and **severely sight impaired** may be used, as these are the currently accepted terms used on the certificate of vision impairment. These both replace, but are synonymous with, 'partially sighted' and 'blind'.

◆ Reference may also be made to **tactile learners**. These children are unable to draw any visual information and are dependent on tactile communication learning methods such as **Braille**, **moon**, on body signing, etc. It does not necessarily preclude the use of speech. References to children with useful vision or residual vision target those who would benefit from increased contrast or well-saturated colours.

◆ **Dual sensory impairment** relates to sight and hearing loss.

◆ **MDVI** stands for **multiple disabilities and vision impairment,** and **MSI** for **multi-sensory impairment.**

◆ **Habilitation training** is the term used for the teaching of orientation and mobility and independent living skills (or life skills) to children and young people with vision impairments.

◆ Anything in **bold** throughout the text can be found in the Glossary.

Part one

Introduction

Introduction

If you have no previous experience, it can be very daunting supporting a child with a vision impairment. You want to do the best for the child, but don't know where to begin. The aim of this handbook is to introduce you to a range of practical activities, skills and strategies which will help a child with vision impairment to be as independent as possible. It is aimed at children of all ages, but specifically targets the Foundation Stage (ages 0–5), with Intermediate and Higher stages to follow. These divisions are artificial, as targets should be stage, not age, appropriate. You should use your own judgement about whether any task is age or ability appropriate or seek guidance from your **habilitation specialist.**

Whilst a number of these skills should be achievable in the Early Years, this does not always happen, and the majority of the tasks and skills in this handbook can also be incorporated into a life skills programme for older children. There are some activities that require greater developmental maturity to provide progression. Chronological age is no indicator of maturity, ability or skill, and for some children delays could stem from factors not related to sight impairment. Bear in mind that there are optimal learning windows for developmental skills. If you miss a window, the skill can still be learned, but it may take longer. Think of it as a roadblock in the brain: it's not insurmountable, it just needs a detour.

The UK Government (2014) published a Code of Practice for organisations who work with and support children and young people with special educational needs and disabilities (SEND), 0 to 25 years which applies in England. They maintain that:

All children and young people are entitled to an education that enables them to:

> ➢ achieve their best;
> ➢ become confident individuals living fulfilling lives; and
> ➢ make a successful transition into adulthood, whether into employment, further or higher education or training.

However, this begins with early, effective intervention and there are not enough specialists to meet this need. With appropriate early intervention, children with vision impairments would achieve the same developmental milestones at the same time as children who are fully sighted (Norris et al. 1957, quoted in Mason and McCall 1997). Vision impairment is regarded as a low incidence, high impact condition. This means that, whilst the numbers are quite low, the specialist teaching, adaptive strategies and devices are time-consuming and expensive. With such a small market, most devices never make it to mass production.

Achieving an appropriate level of independence cannot be valued too highly. Apart from gaining practical skills, learning to undertake independent living tasks improves self-esteem and confidence, and prepares a child for greater involvement in society and the world around them.

There is still a shortage of **registered, qualified habilitation specialists** (RQHS), which cannot be immediately addressed. Therefore, this handbook is intended to set you on your way to supporting children with a vision impairment achieve a variety of independent living skills. It is specifically UK based, so the terminology, services and equipment are relevant and available here. You don't need to read from cover to cover, but rather dip in and out as the need arises.

This handbook primarily targets children and young people with vision impairment. However, a high proportion of the children also have additional disabilities. From personal experience, it has become clear that many of these strategies work equally well with children without a vision impairment who (for whatever reason) have struggled to absorb the necessary skills. Many are particularly suitable for children with autistic spectrum or sensory processing disorders. Much lateral thinking will be needed, because the most obvious way is not always the best. There is no correct way; safety and success are key. Consider each child as an individual and help them achieve as much as they can, safely within their own capabilities.

Most sighted children learn incidentally – that is, by observing their parents and siblings and modelling behaviour. Many exhibit an innate desire to achieve tasks independently. Those who have limited or no vision are at a great disadvantage in the learning process. Without the visual prompt and stimulation, it can be difficult to self-motivate. This is where you come in, as these children need to be specifically taught each of these skills that, with vision, are absorbed effortlessly. Most parents begin encouraging independence from very early on without even realising. Once aware of what you can do, the possibilities are endless!

Bear in mind your aim is to build independence. Your child may need a high level of support and intervention initially, but this should gradually reduce over time as your child learns and takes responsibility for their own development.

BASIC SKILLS AND STRATEGIES YOU WILL NEED

Patience

Repetition of tasks may try the patience of you both. Persevere but try and add in other activities to break monotony, and always try to build in some element of success, even if the entire task cannot be achieved. Don't be afraid to try different techniques if the first one doesn't work.

Never try to introduce tasks when you are short of time. Children tend to work best without time constraints or other pressures. If you are struggling, break the task down into each of its smallest component parts and find a way of working on them first.

Praise and encouragement

Focus on the good. Make it easy for the child to succeed, don't set them up for failure. Prepare the task well and, as the child succeeds and gains confidence, you can either gradually withdraw your assistance or add to the task, making it more challenging. Consider trying new tasks yourself, blindfolded. Consider which aspects you might find difficult, then try thinking how your prior knowledge affects your abilities! Encourage the child to share their success with others. Consider the introduction of appropriate rewards and incentives if necessary. Create a 'Can do' rather than a 'Can't do' environment.

Consistency

Once you have found a method or strategy that works for your child, stick to it and encourage everyone else who works with him to work the same way. He will only get confused if different people present different strategies. Use the same correct terminology as far as possible, as this also promotes consistency.

Working at the child's level

This means you physically get on the floor with him if necessary, to make eye contact easier, but also choose activities that are suitable and engaging. You will need a young child to perceive you as playing with them, or participating in their activity. However, an older child must never think you are patronising. For this you may find it useful to have a basic understanding of child physical, motor and sensory development. You may not think twice about sitting at home with your own child singing nursery rhymes, but for some this can seem intimidating with an audience. Simple songs and rhymes increase learning and add enjoyment: 'The early years of life provide a foundation for all later learning … If teaching is aimed at the child's developmental level, then effective learning will result' (Blythe 2005).

Communication

Choose methods of communication suitable for your child. That means choosing language he will understand – babies and toddlers respond best to higher pitches and exuberance. Babies can recognise their mothers by their scent. If there could be any confusion, address the child by name – a good habit to get into. If you are not immediate family, introduce yourself. Wearing the same bracelet, watch or other jewellery item, provides tactile identity reinforcement. Some people go as far as using the same perfume or body spray. These and similar strategies also work well with children on the autistic spectrum. It is no fun trying to guess who you are talking to when you can't see. Think how you might feel if you met someone out of context and couldn't remember their name.

Poems, songs and rhymes all add enjoyment and make learning more memorable. Remember: you really can hear a smile in your tone of voice. Children with severe sight impairment, like those on the autistic spectrum, require clear instructions. Avoid idiomatic use of language and if specialist terminology or jargon is necessary, be prepared to explain. If you had no prior awareness, think what the phrase 'It's raining cats and dogs!' conjures. Would *you* want to go outside?

Your child is likely to be very dependent on verbal description and instruction, so help him to build his skills. If you have any concerns, seek a referral to a **speech and language therapist.** Contrary to popular belief, those with sight impairment do not have super hearing. They do have brain capacity to make good use of listening skills and draw more information from auditory sources, though. However, good listening skills and concentration need to be taught.

If your child needs **objects of reference**, try to build progression into the objects you choose. For instance, choose a toilet roll, rather than a nappy, to indicate the toilet. Progress can take some time, but you want objects of reference to promote the idea of greater independence and be age appropriate as your child matures.

ONE SIZE DOESN'T FIT ALL

If at first you don't succeed, try a different way! Recognise that there is no set way of doing things. There may be tried-and-tested ways that work with most children, but your child is unique. As long as he is safe

> IF AT FIRST YOU DON'T SUCCEED, TRY, TRY, TRY AGAIN.

and successful, the 'how' doesn't matter. Achieving success at the first attempt is not the norm. Trying again builds resilience. After all, 'FAIL' stands for '**F**irst **A**ttempt **I**n **L**earning'! We all have to overlearn things. We need to do them over and over again until we get the whole process right without breaking it down into component parts or even thinking about it at all. Some children may need more practice than others.

When to seek help

Every child is different, and some have complex conditions and medical needs that must be taken into consideration. Find out as much as possible about any conditions the child has, and what potential effects they may have on their development. If you have any concerns, don't be afraid to ask other professionals for help and guidance.

Many different teaching skills and strategies are explained in more detail in the Glossary (pages 223–235). These include **demonstration, forward chaining, backward chaining, hand over hand, hand under hand, verbal directions, scaffolding**, or a combination of any of these. The Glossary also contains contact details for specialist organisations and charities that may offer resources, support or advice.

THE IMPORTANCE OF PLAY

Children learn through play. It is an essential part of child development and provides a means by which you can identify the stage a child is at. Play gives the child a chance to rehearse scenarios and build an understanding of the world.

According to the World Health Organization (WHO), play is defined as being for its own sake (without a specific goal), voluntary, enjoyed by participants and imaginative. It can be solitary or social, and with or without objects. Young children acquire and consolidate developmental skills through playful interactions with people and objects.

Modern society has changed expectations for children. Children are generally left to their own devices less often. Parents and carers seek to entertain and 'make memories' with their children. Fewer children have day-to-day responsibilities within the household. 'Their own devices' have become electronic ones. This is not to dismiss the value of electronic devices entirely – they have great entertainment value and offer amazing access for children and young people with vision impairment – but movement is vital to development and boisterous play also needs to be encouraged. See Sections 5.00 and 6.00 'Movement' and 'Concept development' and the recommendations for further reading on pages 237–238.

You can enhance understanding and develop concepts through play, without your child noticing. Think about playing trains together. If you ask questions or provide a commentary, action and language combine to build understanding. 'The train is going up and over the bridge.'

And, finally, don't feel obliged to buy expensive specialist toys and equipment. There are plenty available on the high street. Children love attention, so dig out those nursery rhymes from your own childhood, because they offer a wonderful way to interact with your child and mask all the teaching that is happening!

Check the later sections on activities and story bags for ideas, including using a cardboard box!

BASIC DEVELOPMENTAL SKILLS YOUR CHILD WILL NEED

In order to achieve, your child will need these skills at each relevant developmental stage:

➢ Body awareness.

➢ Gross motor skills.

➢ Fine motor skills.

➢ Dexterity and manipulation.

➢ Spatial awareness.

➢ Sensory development.

➢ Appropriate understanding of his environment.

➢ Communication.

➢ Comprehension/understanding of the task.

➢ Cooperation.

It is not possible to cover all these in detail, so it may be worth obtaining a good child development book if you are unsure of any of these areas. There are recommendations in the Further reading section (pages 237–238).

Body awareness

Body awareness is difficult when you cannot see. Use activities like bathtime to increase body awareness, and to draw attention to body parts, limbs and movement. Use massage to increase awareness of hands and fingers and to show how they bend and flex. Fasten Velcro® rattles and bells to ankles and wrists, so movement is rewarded by sound. All babies are fascinated by their own image – even with a severe vision impairment, many will still be able to see themselves in a mirror. Provide a safety mirror that your child can get close to. Good lighting and maybe magnification (depending on the type of vision your child has) may make it more accessible. And, when he is ready, give your child a cardboard box to play in. There's nothing better for helping a child realise how he fits into a space.

For progression, draw round your child on the back of some old wallpaper. Then cut out the shape and decorate it together. This will give your child a rough idea of his size and shape.

For a child with severe sight impairment, the hands provide the window to the world. Therefore, good hand and finger development enables a child to extract the maximum amount of information.

Gross motor skills

Gross motor skills are included here, because if they are good they form the basis of fine motor skills. Where these are underdeveloped, there will be fine motor problems, too. As a parent/carer or specialist practitioner, it is vital that you liaise with other involved professionals, such as occupational therapists, physiotherapists and paediatricians. This will inform your intervention, avoid contraindications and get the best level of care and support for the child.

In order to successfully achieve the tasks in this handbook, your child will need to develop neck and shoulder strength as well as core stability (if not already in place). **Tummy time** is essential, even if your child hates it. It will also develop leg strength, as your child pushes up onto all fours and eventually starts to crawl. Many sighted children are not ready for school because they have missed vital developmental phases. A general reduction in physical activity and gross motor risk taking is responsible for this. There are increasing concerns about children's sedentary lifestyle and dependence on screen time (rather than engaging in boisterous play).

Your child will also need to develop **core stability**, so he has the strength and muscle tone to sit, stand and move around.

Encouraging fine motor skills

Fine motor skills refer to movements and actions of the hands and fingers. This includes:

➢ Recognition of and isolation of individual fingers, e.g. to poke and press.

➤ Hand and finger stability and strength.

➤ Bilateral coordination, using left and right hands together.

➤ Eye and hand coordination.

➤ Types of grasps, e.g. palmar, grasped in the palm of the hand; pincer (forefinger and thumb); tripod (index, middle finger and thumb).

➤ In-hand manipulation (being able to tuck little objects into the fingers and shuffle them away).

➤ Motor planning (being able to adapt to the new or changing demands of movements or actions, including coping with timed or sequenced movements).

If your child is going to be a tactile learner, it is important to develop hand and finger skills and strength.

Activities

Finger isolation and recognition

➤ Make story bags to enhance your child's enjoyment of a story, but get them to hunt for the correct prop in the bag.

➤ Treasure Island. Show an object to the child and then, without them looking, hide the object in a tub of sand/sandpit. See if they can recognise and describe the object before it is revealed.

➤ Put a selection of everyday objects with different textures in a bag, e.g. fork, sandpaper, cotton wool. Let the child identify the items by feeling them in the bag.

➤ Create a sensory treasure box, containing a wide range of different natural textures, feathers, shells, wood etc all covered by rice. The RNIB produces a wonderful leaflet on treasure boxes (www.rnib.org.uk/health-social-and-education-professionals/education-professionals/teaching-and-learning-guidance).

➤ Play hand action rhymes together.

Finger dexterity

➤ Play with pegboards and small pegs. Copy patterns (they may need to be tactile or high-contrast).

➤ Play with playdough, shaving cream, sand, etc.

➢ Spoon from one vessel to another. Vary size weight and density. Wet sand sticks to a spoon, whereas dry sand flows.

➢ Use **Wikki Stix®** or pipe cleaners.

➢ Do finger painting. Put a different colour of paint on each fingertip and make colourful paintings with lines and dots.

➢ Tear paper into small pieces and roll them into balls. You can use these balls to make collages.

➢ Play bashing pegs into board, progressing to Pop-Up Pirate!, or play games such as Operation or Bed Bugs if a child has enough vision.

➢ Sorting out small objects into colours, shapes, sizes.

➢ Extend your range of finger action rhymes ('Tommy Thumb', 'Two Little Dickie Birds', etc.).

➢ Make or buy finger puppets for thumb, index finger and middle finger. Do action rhymes or play finger games/stories that require the fingers to move separately and together. Finger puppets can make the fingers be seen more easily.

➢ Encourage the child to play a musical instrument. The sound provides gratification for the finger movement.

➢ Roll coins, small balls, throw dice, then recover them.

➢ Coins – post into a money box or piggy bank. See if the child can retrieve them.

➢ Play with a jack-in-the-box – traditional toys have stayed around for a good reason. As well as finger dexterity, a jack-in-the-box adds an element of surprise and anticipation to play.

Using both hands together

Bilateral hand use is using two hands together to grasp and manipulate objects. It starts with bringing the hands together at the midline. Eventually, one hand will become dominant. It is important to encourage passing an object from one hand to the other.

➢ Start with clapping games and action rhymes like 'Wind the Bobbin Up'. If your child is not doing this spontaneously, use the hand over hand method (see Glossary, page 227).

➢ Play with a balloon. Choose a strong colour and put some grains of rice inside it, or perhaps a little bell. The child will have to use two hands to hold a balloon.

➢ Give your child two-handled beakers.

➤ Introduce musical toys or noisy toys to bang together, so success is rewarded. Tambourines, drums and maracas all work well. However, spoons and a pan can be just as effective.

➤ Splash hands in the bath.

Progression:

➤ Playdough. Show the child how to make a ball. Roll the ball into a sausage using two hands.

➤ Threading activities. Give the child a shoelace and some beads. Make sure the beads will thread easily. Can she make a pattern on the lace with the beads? Make sure she is using both hands in this activity. Progress to threading smaller beads, buttons, pasta shapes, cotton reels, etc. or to making jewellery on elasticated thread.

➤ Play with construction kits with bricks, nuts and bolts or interlocking pieces. Building toys and construction toys – such as Duplo, blocks, boxes are all useful activities to encourage the child to build using two hands, or each hand separately. The next step would be to try Lego®, K'Nex®, Stickle Bricks® or Popoids®, which all need to be pushed together with more dexterity and force.

➤ Playdough. Show the child how to cut up a playdough sausage, using their knife and fork for fun. Contrast the dough with the surface or plate. Progress to making smaller sausages with their fingers, and making little peas by rolling the dough in their fingers. Aim to make little peaks in the dough using their index finger, middle finger and thumb.

➤ Make paper chains.

➤ Use stencils and templates. Use Blu Tack® to hold stencil in place, if necessary.

➤ Use scissors to make collages, mosaics, etc. Investigate which scissors are best for your child. There is a huge range on the market.

➤ Draw around cardboard shapes. Try making patterns and pictures. Put thick dark lines or tactile markings on card or heavier-weight paper to guide your vision impaired child. Alternatively, look out for embossing tools or stick something onto the paper. You may need to draw a line from the edge of the card to the object you want him to cut out.

➤ Art activities. Print using blocks, sponges, little cars, cotton reels and/or leaves. Give the child wool and junk to make a collage. Let them paint with a chubby brush or dip string into the paint to drop onto the paper.

➤ Do colouring or drawing on small pieces of paper. This encourages the child to stabilise the paper with their non-dominant hand.

Finger strength

➢ Pop bubble wrap. Get people to save packaging for you, or you can buy it on a roll from stationers.

➢ Punch holes into paper using a hole punch or craft punch.

➢ Cut cardboard with a pair of scissors. Try making mosaic patterns. Use the strategies above to assist low vision children.

➢ Play with squirty bottles.

➢ Play with playdough. Pinch, pull, roll, squeeze and cut.

➢ Play with stress relievers or stretchy toys. You can make your own with rubber gloves filled with different textures. Try ordinary flour and cornflour (which has a gelatinous feel).

➢ Peg or hang out dolls' clothes on a line or clothes airer.

➢ Cooking – mixing, sifting, kneading or use of a rolling pin or cutters. Get your child involved in making playdough.

➢ At bathtime, load a sponge with water, then squeeze it out.

➢ If you can, obtain an old-style wipes tub (rather than a box). Clean it out and then fill it with different colours and textures of materials and ribbons, all knotted together. As you pull the material, there will be resistance on each knot as it pulls through the opening.

Hand strength and control

Look for connective or construction toys that need an element of force to join or separate, or stacking toys that need delicate control to avoid knocking them over.

Pushing and pulling games strengthen hands arms and shoulders. As a starting point, use rhymes like 'Row, Row, Row Your Boat'.

When your child starts nursery, he will need arm strength to get through doors, and for Brailling (if he's a tactile learner).

Hammering toys are good. Select sturdy toys with bright contrasting colours if your child has some vision. Plastic or wooden is fine, but (if possible) use it to reinforce colour, shape and texture. Remember: plastic generally all feels the same.

Right from the outset, Montessori nurseries use specially constructed real things. They place a strong emphasis on natural materials, which offer a wealth of textures and help to build descriptive language. Sometimes less is more. There is nothing wrong with allowing your child to play with an old pan and a wooden spoon! It encourages coordination, builds anticipation, demonstrates action and consequence, makes a lovely noise, and it also lets your child feel he is helping in the kitchen.

STORYTELLING

Young children love listening to stories. Don't worry if she asks for the same book over and over again. Include different voices and lots of intonation. A child with a vision impairment is highly dependent on listening skills. Reading to children from an early age builds a love of reading, and develops language, comprehension and complex concepts – all wrapped in a highly entertaining package. Silly voices and rude noises all add to the fun.

If you don't feel confident reading out loud, you can also use YouTube for ideas and reassurance. Try Michael Rosen reading *We're Going on a Bear Hunt* (https://youtu.be/ytcOU2WAz4s) or look on the National Literacy Trust website (www.wordsforlife.org.uk/) for other stories and rhymes to use with your child. You may also find Language Launchpad a useful resource: www.ouh.nhs.uk/languagelaunchpad/

Perhaps add an extra dimension to storytime by using **ClearVision** books, which all have Braille, print and pictures. This allows children with little or no sight to share books with their sighted friends and family (www.clearvisionproject.org/).

MAKE YOUR OWN STORY BAGS!

As well as enhancing the story, story bags can help with the delivery of many different concepts and can provide opportunities to develop coordination and fine motor skills.

For example, three different teddies and a doll are a brilliant start for *Goldilocks and the Three Bears*.

In this story, you can explore big and little, tall and small, keeping yourself safe and respect for others.

Appendix 4 contains story bag ideas (see pages 218–222).

SORTING

Sorting is a really useful activity. You can build visual and tactile discrimination, as well as learning more about specific things and developing fine motor skills. Take the opportunity to use items in a range of colours, sizes, textures and weights.

Make your own sorting tray

Save the inserts from biscuit or cake selection packs. If they seem dark or offer poor contrast, add coloured paper into each compartment or section.

If your child is sorting cutlery, they can sort directly into your cutlery drawer. While this is great in terms of taking on chores and responsibilities, for some children it may prove too complex or a bit daunting.

If you do not have an old cutlery tray available, they can be purchased in pound shops, or else in inexpensive hardware stores. They can be used for a range of things, and help to keep everything together and within reach. Takeaway containers are another sorting option, but ideally things are best kept together on a tray.

Smaller items can be sorted in an eggbox, from another container. This activity works well with coins.

Household items useful for sorting

> Buttons – organise by colour, size, texture.

> Coins – before sorting into value, try separating coins from other things, or splitting them into copper and silver.

> Cutlery – sort by type or size or texture, or match into sets, in preparation for moving onto bigger cutlery or setting the table.

> Toy cars.

> Smarties or jelly beans.

Note: Never leave children alone with anything they might swallow.

Part two

Habilitation skills: Foundation skills (Early Years) curriculum

1.00–2.00: Dressing, undressing and fastenings

1.00	Dressing
	Undressing
1.01	Shoes off
1.02	Socks off
1.03	Joggers off
1.04	Coat off
1.05	Top/T-shirt off
1.06	Dress off
	Dressing
1.08	Identify own coat
1.09	Socks on
1.10	Shoes on – correct feet
1.11	Joggers on
1.12	Coat on
1.13	Top/T-shirt on
1.14	Dress on
1.15	Clothing on right way up, right way round
2.00	Fastenings
2.01	Poppers
2.02	Buttons
2.03	Velcro®
2.04	Zip closed
2.05	Zip open-ended

Activities to work on these skills

Busy Bags: 4 Sock skills, 13a Tying shoelaces part 1

Activity Sheets: 1 I can fasten 1, I can fasten 2

Progression: Activity Sheet 3 I can look after my clothes, Busy Bag 13b Tying shoelaces part 2

To work on prerequisite skills

Refer to discussion of body awareness, body parts, finger separation and manual dexterity – fine motor development in the Introduction (pages 7–12).

Busy Bags: 3 Peg and pompom making, 6 Bath paint

Activity: 1 Songs and rhymes

Handout: 8 10 simple ways to work on balance skills

Handouts

4 Dressing tricks and tips, 16 Daily living skills activities for preschool children

Useful websites

➤ Tying shoes (for strugglers): https://mommyevolution.com/how-to-tie-a-shoe-step-by-step/

➤ Tying shoes ('bunny ears' method): https://raisingchildren.net.au/preschoolers/health-daily-care/dressing/shoelaces

➤ Tying shoes (four ways): www.wikihow.com/Tie-Your-Shoes

UNDRESSING: 1.01–1.06

Even the smallest baby seems to be able to remove socks and bootees at will. This is the skill that you need to develop if you want your child to be able to dress independently. You will want your child to be as independent as possible before starting nursery or school. This will boost his confidence. Remember: dressing skills are usually acquired through observation and copying. The lower your child's vision, the more direct intervention and skill-teaching he will require. Use fun and games to keep your child engaged.

Your child will need to develop their motor skills to become competent at dressing and undressing. Lots of motor activities will contribute to improving dressing and undressing.

Always begin with undressing. The very thing that drives you mad – encourage and praise! Taking off socks, hats and gloves is a necessary precursor to dressing skills. It is easier to pull clothes off than to calculate how to put something on. Socks, gloves and hats require little effort to remove. Other clothing tends to require a higher skillset.

Make it easier by selecting clothing without fasteners. Joggers and leggings are great, and will be essential when it comes to potty training.

Zips slide more easily by adding zip pulls. These are commercially available, but if not a hair bobble or paper clip will suffice to offer a child a bigger area to grasp. Once he can undo the zip, your child will be able to shrug his coat off. Buttons require greater dexterity, so help with buttons initially and then allow him to succeed with removing the coat. Ensure you child has a sense of achievement and success.

During this learning period, try to avoid clothing with tight necks. Getting a top stuck over your head can be quite traumatic!

DRESSING: 1.08–1.15

Always allow plenty of time. If you are rushing, it will become stressful for both of you.

Introduce systematic procedures early on. For instance, teach 'magic hands' and pull hands back up coat sleeves, to prevent turning it inside out. This makes putting the coat back on again much easier. This is really helpful if your child puts his coat on and off at playschool or nursery. Sometimes it can be very difficult to tell if a coat is inside out when you can't see.

The same system is enormously helpful when dressing and undressing for PE. Encourage clothes to be placed carefully on a chair, rather than left where they drop. All children lose bits and pieces of PE kit, but this is much more likely when you can't see. The system can be further developed so that clothes for the next day can be placed ready for morning. When the child is more proficient at dressing alone, lay his clothes out on the chair in the order he needs to put them on.

Coats come on and off several times a day, so it is good to target them early on. Break the task down into small components and let the child do the bit they are most likely to succeed in. Quite often, this would be the final pulling up of the zip, reinforcing the idea of successful completion. You can then add more and more into the child's task, using **backward chaining** or **scaffolding** to ensure the child continues to complete the task successfully.

Hood Technique

There are always a number of different ways of undertaking each task. Placing the hood on your head is one of the easiest ways to put a coat on. The hood holds the coat in place whilst the child can use both hands to get the arms in. A button into the top of the hood helps with centring.

Zips are easy to undo, but locating an open-ended zip can be difficult. Again, bigger, plastic zips are easier than those with small metal teeth and a colour contrast with the coat will also help.

Buy an extra-large zip for practice. Alternatively, purchase a couple of different-coloured large zips and swap the colours round so that they contrast better.

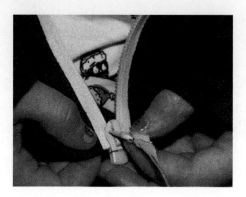

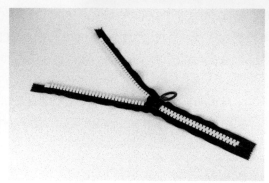

Montessori nurseries are based on developing relevant practical skills and techniques. Many of their strategies work well when supporting children with vision impairment, as they rely on doing rather than watching. Teaching children to put coats on is one such skill. Here the open coat is placed on the floor, neckline towards the body. The child can put both arms into the sleeves, without having to hold the coat. Arms in, the coat is lifted up and over the head. Try it: it really does work! It also works when seated, as well as being a great way of putting a coat on when in a wheelchair.

Montessori flip

As an alternative, place the coat on the floor the same way and allow the child to lie on their back on the open coat and slide their arms into the sleeves. For some, this method just makes the most sense. Once they have the understanding, it is not usually a problem to adopt more traditional techniques.

Once your child starts school, clothes selection may be more restricted. Smaller school trousers are often available with elasticated waists. There are pros and cons for cardigans, fleeces and sweatshirts, but, if dressing is an issue, try to be consistent until the first style of garment is mastered. With sweatshirts, put arms in first. This reduces time spent struggling to get the head through the neck.

Place the sweatshirt face down on a table, with the waistband over the edge and closest to the child. It is easier to identify the front if it has a logo. If not, use the label or sew in a small button. Push the arms in and keep going until the child's hands appear at the sleeves. With his hands free, it is quick and easy to lift the neck of the garment over the head and then push the head through.

Tricks and tips

➢ Mix and match activities. Look for tasks and games that develop motor skills, particularly those around fine motor hand movements necessary to prepare for dressing.

➢ Velcro® is great, and a good starting point. However, new Velcro® sometimes needs a great deal of force to separate the two sides, or as it ages it can get so clogged with fluff it no longer grips. Use a fine-toothed comb to tease the threads out.

➢ Big buttons are easier than small buttons, as long as the buttonholes are large enough. Colour-contrast button and material for practice. If you have a crafty friend or relative, see if they can create a button-fastening activity. The example on the previous page is made from strips of felt with contrasting buttons.

➢ A small button in the inside top back of clothing helps ensure clothes are the right way up and right way round. Label locations are not reliable enough. Some labels can pose a problem to children with sensory issues, so a degree of lateral thinking may be required.

➢ Use a zip pull to make it easier for the child to slide the zip up or down. You can buy them quite cheaply online or you can buy character ones to engage the child. Alternatively, you can just loop a hair bobble through.

➢ For teaching purposes, look for a bold contrast between zip teeth and the fabric of the zip. You can buy zips of different colours and mix and match. This will make both the teeth and process more visible. Bigger zips are easier to manipulate and to learn how to use.

➢ Suggest appropriate clothing, such as joggers or elasticated shorts. Opt for clothing items that are stretchy and/or not too tight.

➢ Start off sitting down to pull joggers on, as balancing on one leg makes the process much more difficult. Tie in undressing with potty training or toileting skills.

➢ When your child grows out of his coat, try to avoid buying one that is significantly different, as this may require a new skillset.

➢ Hoods on coats provide a great starting point. A furry hood, or a button inside, helps the child know the coat is the right way up.

➢ Suggest that your child's school or nursery make his coat peg easily accessible (perhaps on the end of the row). Also, request bright, bold or tactile signage to identify the peg.

➢ Shoelaces are a difficult skill for all children to acquire. Therefore, learning this is best left until other dressing skills are secure. However, the prerequisite skills – like developing the pincer grip and threading – can be introduced with a view to tying laces when your child is ready.

➢ There is always more than one way to do something!

Dressing resources to consider buying

Toys change rapidly. These suggestions are all currently available, but if you see something you think would be useful, buy it! You may not see it again.

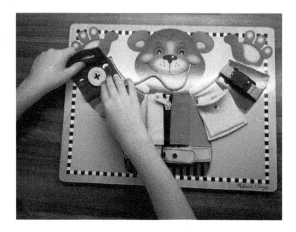

Something like this Melissa & Doug™ fastenings board is easier to manipulate than traditional dressing soft toys. These toys do not often offer an open-ended zip (although this one does), as they can be a real challenge for small children. Melissa & Doug™ toys are always a worthwhile investment.

However, buying a doll that can wear real baby clothes can be an even better investment. Look for a doll that is 45 cm (18 in) tall. If you can get one that is toddler size, you can dress it in football kits to engage as many children as possible. If there is nothing current, look in charity shops. A spell in the freezer will kill most bugs and the washer or dishwasher can be surprisingly successful at cleaning dolls up. The best dolls for dressing purposes have soft bodies, so it will have to dry out afterwards! Make sure the hair is carefully tied up beforehand, however! Alternatively, add to the learning experience by letting the child bathe the doll. As a rough guide, a correctly proportioned 60 cm (24 in) baby doll fits three-month baby clothes, which can be obtained relatively cheaply. We use dolls that wear nine- to twelve-month baby clothes.

As well as practical skill activities, look for toys like jigsaws or wooden dress-up sets that develop sequencing and matching. Here, again, it can be worth visiting charity shops or searching local Facebook selling pages.

There are several useful books that support learning about dressing:

➢ *Scruffy Teddy Gets Dressed*, by Jill Harker (Parragon).

➢ *Getting Ready*, by Child's Play (International).

➢ *We Can Get Dressed: Putting on My Clothes*, by Marion Cocklico (Campbell Books).

2.00: FASTENINGS

Progression

 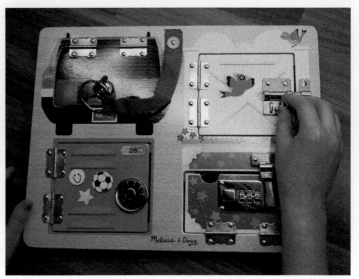

You can progress onto more complex fastenings. Manipulation boards can be bought from specialist suppliers, but they are much more expensive and more suited to older children. Melissa & Doug™ produce a fantastic range of portable wooden manipulation toys at reasonable prices.

Tying laces

Laces can be introduced when the child is ready, but bear in mind that sighted children are usually around six before they can successfully tie them. Although there are lots of ways to avoid shoelaces, tying bows is useful for many other things. Here, again, there are a number of different ways of tying bows. More details can be found in the Tips and tricks below. There are a number of no-tie lace alternatives (if preferred), which are also listed below.

How many different ways do you know to tie laces? There are two basic styles. Within these two methods, there are many different adaptations, to try to make children more successful.

Have a look at Busy Bag 13, parts a and b (pages 125–129). Don't forget: the child will need good dexterity and fine motor skills (even more than the other dressing skills), so work on those, too.

Traditional loop and wrap (around the tree)

See www.wikihow.com/Tie-Your-Shoes for all these techniques.

Work alongside or behind your child. Mirroring the technique is very difficult.

Bunny ears

Also known as the chocolate box bow, this is often the easiest for children. The Busy Bags and Tips and tricks have more details, or take a look at the weblink above.

The advantage of the bunny ears method is that it uses the same basic knot twice.

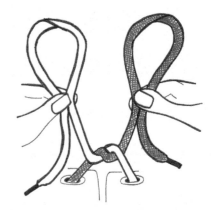

One-handed lace tying

www.tmcsea.org/uploads/1/3/9/8/13988756/one_handed_shoe_tying.pdf

If your child has limited use of one hand, this technique works well, but requires a degree of useful vision.

Remember: when learning to tie laces, use two laces with different colours or that have different textures. This makes it easier to differentiate between the two.

Tricks and tips

➢ In order to be able to succeed in tying laces, your child will need to be able to thread a lace through eyelets, and have a good pincer grip. If laces prove troublesome, consider working on a variety of fine motor skills. Busy Bags 13a and b (pages 125–129) offer lacing and tying activities.

➢ While being able to tie shoelaces is no longer essential, failure to master the task can reduce choices and cause embarrassment later. It can be a particular problem for boys as they start to move into adult-size shoes and Velcro® trainers become scarce and/or expensive.

➢ Make sure the laces are not too long. The child needs to hold the lace close to the knot, as holding the aglet (the sheath around the end of the lace) seems to draw children's fingers.

➢ Begin with two different colours and/or two different textures or weaves of lace. This reduces confusion as to which lace is which.

➤ Wired ribbon also works well, as the wire helps keep the loops in position. Alternatively, you can start off with pipe cleaners. Make sure they contrast well with the shoe and consider two different colours to start with.

➤ Break the task down and just concentrate on one element, starting with the first cross or knot.

➤ If using a shoe, make sure the toe points away from the child. (It can be difficult if practised in reverse.) Bring the laces close to the child. Don't start with the shoes on their feet.

➤ Mix and match activities. As an alternative, try fastening an apron or tying a bow on a present. Always start by tying aprons off at the front, rather than behind.

NO-TIE LACE ALTERNATIVES

If your child really cannot get the hang of tying laces – there really are lots of options with slip-ons or Velcro®, as well as different tying techniques – then you may like to consider a no-tie alternative. There are a number of different products, some more suitable for certain types of footwear or circumstances than others. You can buy elastic laces that look like traditional laces but stretch, or you can consider some of the following:

➤ For boots or sports trainers, look for quick elastic laces with locks.

➤ Try curly laces or kids' smart silicone laces for casual trainers or shoes. Silicone laces slot through eyelets and require no fastening at all. Hickies are the brand leader in silicone laces, but require some dexterity to fit. Many cheaper alternatives are available.

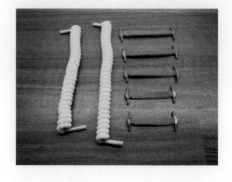

3.00: Personal hygiene

3.00	PERSONAL HYGIENE
	Toileting
3.01	Locate potty
3.02	Sit on potty
3.03	Locate toilet at home
3.04	Locate toilet in educational setting
3.05	Understand use of toilet/potty appropriately
3.06	Wash hands
3.07	Dry hands
3.08	Wash face
3.09	Brush teeth
3.10	Supported bathing/showering

Activities to work on these skills

Busy Bag: 11 Brushing teeth
Activity Sheets: 1 I can fasten 1, 2 I can fasten 2, 4 Hand-washing

Prerequisite skills

Refer to discussion of body awareness, body parts, finger separation, bilateral hand use and manual dexterity – fine motor development in the Introduction (pages 7–12), plus 1.00–2.00, 'Dressing, undressing and fastenings' (pages 17–26).

Activity: 1 Songs and rhymes

Handouts

5 This Is the Way We Brush Our Teeth and Wash, Wash, Wash Your Hands, 16 Daily living skills activities for preschool children

3.01–3.05: TOILETING

Children become ready for toilet training at different times. For a child with severe sight impairment it is likely that the absence of incidental learning – being able to see others using a potty or toilet – will further delay their readiness. By contrast, some may be so distressed by soiling themselves that they push for early training. There are plenty of publications on the market to assist with the process, but nothing specifically geared to vision impairment. If you are experiencing difficulties, you may find your **health visitor** or **school nurse** can offer advice. Both teams often contain specialists or can refer you to a more appropriate service. As a rough guide, girls are physically ready earlier than boys, but you are looking at a window somewhere between 18 and 36 months. Toileting programmes change with fashion and greater scientific knowledge, but the most important thing is that it works for your child. If your child cannot maintain a good posture or has other physical needs, a referral to **occupational therapy** or **physiotherapy** may help.

Physical readiness is shown by:

➢ Being able to walk, stand and sit.

➢ Indicating some elements of bladder control – for instance, going longer without urinating, or having a dry nappy after three hours.

➢ An awareness of bodily functions – for instance, child stops playing or squats to pass water or faeces.

Mental/emotional readiness is shown by:

➢ Showing interest in others using a toilet.

➢ Announcing when she has had a wee or a poo.

➢ Shows interest in using the potty or toilet.

So you can talk about the toileting process, you will need a name for your child's genitals. Current thinking is that children should be encouraged to use the correct terminology, but many parents are not comfortable with this. In the early stages, it is more important that each body part has a name and the functions are understood. You may well find that correct terminology is introduced when your child starts school. Euphemisms have been discouraged to ensure common understanding and clarity in the event of any abuse taking place. (If you want to know more about this, look up **protective behaviours** in the Glossary, or go to www. protectivebehaviours.org/what-does-protective-behaviours-mean). Establish what you will call everything associated with the toilet and stick to it. Get everyone who works with your child to use the same terminology.

If you are not the child's parent or carer, you must ensure that you are fully aware of, and comply with, all appropriate safeguarding procedures. You have a duty to protect yourself as well as the child. Your employer or voluntary organisation should have a code of practice and safeguarding procedures, and training should be delivered regularly. The Dos and Don'ts below are directly primarily at parents and carers, and safeguarding procedures need to be applied by others.

Do

✓ Take your child into the toilet with you. If they get used to going in with you, they will start to associate the bathroom with activities like toileting. The bathroom/toilet is a unique environment in the home. The lack of soft furnishings makes it echo and feel bigger than it is. Even running water sounds different.

✓ Bribery (in any form) rules! Keep a packet of Smarties or similar on hand. Or use taped songs or favourite toys – anything that constitutes a reward.

✓ Use the same routine every time when entering and leaving the toilet. Think about a simple route in and out, and add any tactile points in the room that the child may understand (bells on the door, elastic band on the handle, for example).

✓ Provide activities in the bathroom, particularly if the child is slow to pass a motion or is inclined towards constipation.

✓ Be flexible about the use of the potty or toilet. Gaining good bladder and bowel control is more important than whether they use the toilet or the potty.

✓ Use the flush system as a reward. Most children love to hear it and do it for themselves. If your child uses the potty, empty it in the toilet and let your child flush before washing her hands.

✓ Put toilet roll within reach.

✓ Be sure the child always does the whole process, including handwashing, every time.

✓ Make a huge fuss about every success.

Don't

✗ Make a big fuss about accidents – and there will be many! Take the child to the bathroom to change her wet clothes, so that the act becomes associated with the appropriate places.

✗ Try and push your child to use the toilet rather than the potty. A lot of vision impaired children fear sitting on a toilet – it is, after all, a long drop. Do not leave them on their own, and always offer lots of talk and support such as holding hands. Singing aloud helps, too!

✘ Some children need to 'look' at what they have done and where it is, so don't be too squeamish about it. However, it can be discouraged as the child develops the skill.

✘ Stop your little boy playing with his penis (well, except in public!). It's a natural part of finding out about his body and its functions.

✘ Don't use a nappy as an **object of reference**. Choose something more progressive, such as toilet roll or pants.

Tips and tricks

➢ Invest in a **RADAR Key** (disabled toilet key) for when you are out and about There is usually more space, and restricted access can mean it is cleaner than other public toilets. This will stand you in good stead when your older child wants to go to the toilet independently when you are out.

➢ If your child uses a potty, always return it to the same place (ideally, the toilet or bathroom). Make sure that the potty will not slide away as your child goes to sit on it. Dycem® mat or equivalent will work (it can go into a hot wash afterwards). It also affords an opportunity to provide contrast between the potty and the floor. Bear in mind your child is likely to leave it to the last minute to find the potty.

➢ To reduce fear, allow your child to explore and learn about the toilet (many children fear the toilet, not just those with vision impairment). Consider it for a moment from the perspective of a child with no vision – the idea of being lifted up to sit precariously perched above a great big bottomless bowl where the water might gush down at any point, pulling you with it. Exploration of the toilet and how it works may reduce this anxiety. Opt for a toilet seat that contrasts with the bowl. While white on white looks clean and modern, it all merges together if you have reduced vision. To encourage independence and security and put control back in your child's hands, get a toilet step or a combined step and seat. If your child has useful vision, look for a bright contrasting colour. Make sure that any child seat or insert fits well and doesn't move around. Consult with other parents, to see what has worked best for them.

➢ Good positioning can help your child feel safe and also help him pass a motion more easily. Don't let his feet swing in the air. Provide a stool where he can rest his feet securely. As well as improving his position, it will make him feel more secure and offer resistance to push against if he needs to strain. Ideally the hip should be angled upwards, so not at 90 degrees. Your child will adopt this position naturally on the potty. If he doesn't seem to grasp the straining idea, try getting him to blow bubbles, which uses all the same muscles.

➢ You are aiming towards independence, so make sure toilet paper is reachable. Many children find wipes easier and it can be easier to control the volume used. However, if you choose the wipes option, do look for genuinely biodegradable wipes –flushable is not the same as biodegradable.

➢ If your child hates the splash from the toilet as they poo, always put a couple of sheets of toilet paper across the surface beforehand.

➢ Some children find the whole idea of passing a motion frightening and may need specialist support. If the fear is so great that they can only poo in a nappy, go with that for a while. They can still sit on the potty or toilet wearing the nappy, then can progress to laying a nappy across the bowl. Seek professional advice if this fear leads to constipation. As mentioned earlier, some **health visitors** and **school nurses** specialise in toileting problems.

➢ Remember: Boys do not have to stand to wee if they don't want to, or find it difficult. Urinals are notoriously difficult to access in strange toilets, so it is perfectly acceptable to go into a cubicle to sit. If he does wish to use a urinal, please explain why it is unacceptable to drop his trousers to urinate in public toilets.

➢ If he wishes to stand at home and has some useful vision, consider putting dark blue loo flush into the cistern to provide a target area. If you are really keen to pursue this line, consider a potty-training urinal with spinning target.

➢ At night, make sure a light stays on, or consider a motion-activated toilet light: you can change the colours, it can help your child orientate himself and it offers a target area.

Useful resources

Both these products shown are currently available on Amazon, but you can also get them from a number of different retailers:

➢ *Bear in the Big Blue House: Potty Time with Bear* [DVD].

➢ *Sesame Street: Elmo's Potty Time* [DVD].

3.06–3.08: WASHING

Remember: you are trying to build independence, so set your bathroom up accordingly.

Make sure the light pull is long enough for your child to turn on independently. Most children with sight impairment have some useful vision, so help her to use it. Choose a cord pull that has substance but is not too heavy, and make sure it contrasts with the surface behind.

Mark up your taps. With small children, it's simplest to indicate the cold tap and tell them to choose that one. Cold water is fine for handwashing – it is the soap, not the temperature of the water, that makes a difference. You can use an elastic band, a bright hair bobble, a pipe cleaner or a Bump on (available from the RNIB) to identify the tap. Finding out about hot and cold is important and has a bearing on later safety. Some taps are more difficult to turn than others, so try together at first. If she really struggles, you can buy tap extensions that give her more leverage – these are often red and blue.

Initially, she will probably need a step to reach the washbasin. Choose one that has rubber feet, so it does not slide across the floor. You want her to feel safe. Try and get one that contrasts with your floor and bathroom suite (strong primary colours are the most visible). A deep-coloured towel is also easier to find, but get everyone into the habit of putting things in the right place, regardless.

Bar or liquid soap is personal choice. However, soap bars can be difficult for small hands to grasp securely. Encourage one press on the liquid soap… but be prepared for more! Introduce the idea of face washing using just warm water to avoid your child becoming averse to the process.

Try to build the skills in your own bathroom before transferring them elsewhere, particularly if your child tends to be overenthusiastic with the use of water and soap! Schools and nurseries offer child-sized washbasins and toilets, which makes it easier.

Use the instructions below and Activity Sheet 4: Hand-washing (page 139) to rehearse hand-washing procedures.

Hand-washing instructions

1   Run the tap until it becomes warm (unless you are just using cold water).

2   Wet your hands by putting them under the tap, then put soap in your hands.

3   Scrub, scrub, scrub – especially between your fingers, the tops of your fingers and under your nails. Don't forget your thumb!

4   Rinse your hands well under the water, making sure to get rid of all the soap.

5   Dry your hands with whatever is available: paper towels, a towel or a hand-drying machine.

6   Turn off the tap.

Wash, Wash, Wash Your Hands
(To the tune of 'Row, Row, Row Your Boat')

Wash, wash, wash your hands,
To get them very clean,
Soap them up and scrub and rub,
Germs are very mean.

Wash, wash, wash your hands,
Let's all sing this twice, Soap them up and scrub and rub,
Being clean is really nice!

3.09: TOOTH-BRUSHING

This Is the Way We Brush our Teeth
(To the tune of 'Here We Go Round the Mulberry Bush')

This is the way we brush our teeth, brush our teeth, brush our teeth,
This is the way we brush our teeth, early in the morning (or 'on our way to bed').

This is the way we brush our teeth, toothpaste on, toothpaste on,
This is the way we brush our teeth, a pea sized blob of toothpaste.

This is the way we brush our teeth, round and round, round and round,
This is the way we brush our teeth, round and round in circles.

This is the way we brush our teeth, front and back, front and back,
This is the way we brush our teeth, till they're clean and sparkly.

This is the way we brush our teeth, two minutes long, two minutes long,
This is the way we brush our teeth, let's hum it through again.

Equipment

Children with sensory issues may find toothbrushes invasive and toothpaste flavours rather strong, so alternative strategies may need to be employed. Soft brushes are best to start with. To maximise visibility, choose a bright, well-saturated coloured brush. For babies, look at the silicone finger brushes/gum massagers. These are available clear or coloured, and introduce your baby to toothbrushing gently, with no risk of jamming the toothbrush to the back of the throat. Babies only need a smear of paste.

Once you allow your child to brush their own teeth, remember that small hands need small tools – and this applies to toothbrushes too. You really don't want a toddler pushing a full-sized toothbrush down their throat. It is recommended that children need help brushing their teeth until about the age of 7. A child with vision impairment or sensory issues may need help for longer, though.

If your child has good useful vision, character toothbrushes may prove attractive. Otherwise, look for good tactile surfaces and perhaps a timer. Two minutes' brushing feels a really long time when you can't see.

You can set a two-minute electronic timer, or perhaps a bright sand timer. Alexa or Google Home both provide good accurate timers, working on voice control. Alternatively, you can sing 'This Is the Way We Brush our Teeth' (see page 33); twice through the song lasts almost two minutes, which is pretty close for a small child.

Children do not need electric toothbrushes, and some may find them disconcerting. However, they can be very attractive to **sensory-seeking** children. Choose a children's toothpaste and pay attention to the flavour your child prefers. Many children dislike mint toothpaste, but there are lots of alternatives. A quick check online reveals strawberry, raspberry, bubblegum, melon, berry and ice cream flavours – all easily obtainable – as well as mild mint. For those proving even more sensitive, unflavoured toothpaste is available. Some of these flavours come in bright colours that contrast beautifully with the bristles. It doesn't matter if your child cannot swap to adult toothpaste. It is more important that he cleans his teeth regularly than uses age appropriate toothpaste. Your dentist can advise if higher fluoride paste would be beneficial.

Tips and tricks

➤ Putting toothpaste onto a brush requires a great deal of coordination and dexterity. Small children with sight impairment are going to struggle. You may also have to contend with oral sensitivity, so it could be a long, slow process getting your child to accept teeth-cleaning.

➤ If you plan to get the child to put toothpaste on the brush, try to ensure the brush is a strong, well-saturated colour and the toothpaste contrasts with the bristles. However, it is easier to squeeze a pea-sized blob of paste onto a finger and then put the paste directly onto teeth. Some people prefer to squirt paste straight onto the teeth – in which case, individual tubes may be preferable. Find a system that works in your household for identifying toothpaste. You can: attach labels with elastic bands; use a hair bobble; or mark a lid up more permanently and swap the lid onto each new tube. Accidentally using a soap product is likely to put anyone off brushing their teeth!

➤ You can buy toothpaste dispensers. This makes it a one-handed task and ensures the tube genuinely contains toothpaste. However, you would still have to learn alternative strategies for when away from home, and it may dispense too much toothpaste at a time for a child.

Useful resources

➤ Elefun & Friends: Crocodile Dentist [game].

➤ *Hey Duggee: The Tooth Brushing Badge* [board book and Prime Video].

➤ *Peppa Pig Dentist Trip* [book].

➤ *Sesame Street: Ready, Set, Brush! A Pop-Up Book*

3.10: BATHING AND SHOWERING

Bathtime is an opportunity for fun and relaxation and strengthens the bond between parent and child. It often forms part of a bedtime routine and acts as a cue that bedtime is coming. Using a scented bath product makes it more of a sensory experience, but all products should be age appropriate. Also avoid stimulating scents and select calming ones such as lavender or camomile.

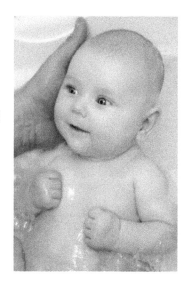

Even a calming bath provides learning opportunities. Take the opportunity to improve your child's body awareness. Washing between her fingers or toes shows her that her fingers separate. Massage the joints to show her that they bend and use rhymes or description to give her the names of the relevant body parts.

If her bath is *not* part of the bedtime routine, you can incorporate all sorts of stimulating activities. Kicking and splashing introduces cause and effect. If she has useful vision, look for a brightly coloured bath foam as well as one with a stimulating scent, or encourage her to draw on her body with bath crayons. For something a little different, take a look at Lush's Fun range, using the Rainbow colours. It can be used as soap, shampoo and bath foam as well as moulded into different shapes.

Remember: While it is important to develop independence, safety is vital. Young children can drown in less than 5 cm (2 in) of water.

4.00: Feeding, eating and drinking

4.00	Feeding
4.01	Finger feeding
4.02	Spoon
4.03	Fork
4.04	Knife
4.05	Training cup
4.06	Straight-sided beaker
4.07	Cup/glass
4.08	Load and spoon from one vessel to another
4.09	Blowing bubbles
4.10	Palmar grip
4.11	Pincer grip
4.12	Tripod grip

Activities to work on these skills

Busy Bags: 2 Edible sensory rattle, 8 Spoon control, 14 Messy play

Progression: Busy Bag 1 LLI (liquid level indicator) – Pouring, Busy Bag 10 Use a whisk – make Angel Delight

Prerequisite skills

Refer to discussion of body awareness, body parts, finger separation, bilateral hand use and manual dexterity – fine motor development in the Introduction (pages 7–12).

Busy Bags: 3 Peg and pompom making, 6 Bath paint

Handouts

6 Supporting cold pouring, 16 Daily living skills activities for preschool children, Cutlery progression guidance (page 42).

4.00: FEEDING

Routine is helpful, as it is with many things. Your child needs to understand what is happening now and what will happen next. Being in the kitchen with you while you cook exposes him to new sounds and smells, and also introduces the idea that food is prepared and cooked and doesn't magically appear.

Small children should sit in a highchair (or similar) to eat, because it indicates to them that food is coming. It also helps to provide a good posture, which improves breathing and swallowing. Inflatable cushioned highchair inserts are useful: to offer optimum support, you gradually let the air out of them as the child grows.

Munchkin plain high ridge suction plate

Most children seem to be able to lift and throw even the best suction plates, so it may be worth putting finger food directly on the tray.

As your child progresses through the stages, consider utensils and plates carefully. Choose a plain single-colour background, as character plates tend to be very 'busy' (if she has some useful vision, it can make it difficult for her to find food on the plate). Also look for a high-ridged side, which can be used to push food against to load the fork or spoon.

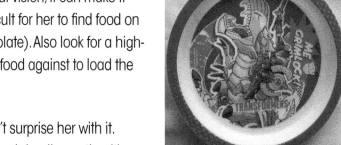

When you first introduce solid food, don't surprise her with it. Tell her it is coming, say what it is and touch her lip gently with the spoon before putting anything into her mouth. If you have concerns about introducing solid food, or your child is resistant, speak with your **health visitor**. If she has difficulty swallowing or gags, you may need a referral to a **speech and language therapist**. Very rarely, children have a condition called **dysphagia**, which is the medical term for difficulty in swallowing, and is very different to resistance to new tastes and textures (which is quite normal).

4.01: FINGER FEEDING

Your baby should be able to sit independently and hold her head up before you introduce finger food. She is likely to be between 9 and 12 months before she is ready and must be more than 6 months old to have the necessary developmental skills. She does not need teeth to eat finger food. Babies may gag if food hits certain areas of the tongue or roof of the mouth; this is a reaction by a sensitive area of the mouth. this is different from choking and does not indicate a food like or dislike. Gagging is only a concern if it is persistent.

Small children tend to grasp with the palmar grip first. However, finger food is the best way to develop the pincer grip: efforts are immediately rewarded with great taste and texture as well as a feeling of success.

Remember: Fingers came first, so don't rush to moving onto using cutlery. Eating a broad range of food with a variety of textures matters more than anything else.

Make sure food is contained within a limited area within her reach – preferably not in a bowl that can be easily upended. Try to provide contrast between the food and the surface or dish, to make it easier to find. Early finger food should be soft inside with defined firmer edges. Initially, avoid foods that are slimy or sloppy, as these are difficult to pick up. Most vegetables will need to be at least partially cooked.

Oral sensitivity textures and taste

Help your baby learn about and build an interest in food through all of her senses, including touch! Allowing her to explore new foods by touch, you're helping to reduce tactile avoidance (defensiveness), foster her interest in food in general and become a more adventurous and healthy eater. And, as she grows, she will start to respond to and organise that sensory input and develop her reflexes. Usually, vision is the primary sensory input that coordinates and integrates the senses. Without it, babies can lack the necessary sensory integration and sensory issues can develop. It can be difficult to tell the difference between sensory issues and autistic spectrum conditions. At this stage, all babies need stimulation – they use it to learn about their world, but it is important to compensate right from the outset for reduced visual input. Incoming sensory information comes in these forms: touch, taste, sound, sight, smells, vestibular input (the body's position in space) and proprioceptive input (sensations from muscles and joints).

Before a baby is born, the sucking and rooting reflex, together with taste buds, are already in place and functioning. The sense of smell is also vital to taste. Children have more taste receptors than adults and strong taste can be overpowering. The tongue moves the food around to identify flavours, and chewing and swallowing enhance flavour and smell. When the tongue recognises the flavour, it sends a message to the brain, which in turn sends a message to the digestive system to release the correct digestive juices. Different textures and resistance require more complex movement of food around the mouth so it can be chewed effectively.

These activities below focus on **touch, taste, sound, sight** and **smell** through simple highchair activities. If your baby is not ready for these activities, try adapting and simplifying them to extend the range of experiences. It is too easy to overprotect a sight impaired baby and not give her the opportunity to properly develop the skill of mastication and swallowing solid food. It is not unusual for children to prefer softer foods, but it is important that they move onto more solid foods at the right time. Always slice grapes or similar foods in half, lengthways, to avoid a choking risk. Consider buying a fresh food feeder, available as mesh or silicone food containers, for baby to chew on. These enable you to offer wider food sensations without the risk, and are available from all good baby retailers.

Tips and tricks

The move from liquids to solids can be challenging for any child, but an infant with a severe vision impairment may really struggle with the concept of chewing. There are a number of strategies you can use to help her.

Let her feel your jaw when chewing. Choose food that will make an audible crunch, and exaggerate your jaw movement while encouraging her to feel both your cheek and under your jaw. Make sure you finish with a swallow. She needs to understand the whole process.

Share your food with her, but ensure it is developmentally appropriate in terms of both size and content. You want to encourage chewing, not put her off or put her at risk. Let her feed you. Sharing is a normal developmental phase and is to be encouraged. Do check that she does actually swallow before allowing her to take more food.

Some crunchy food dissolves in the mouth, so the child needs less developed oral motor skills to cope with successfully, but at the same time, encourages the development of those skills. Crunchy foods make a lovely noise that rewards and reinforces chewing.

➢ Finger foods that dissolve: Cheerios, rice cakes, Rice Krispies, Quavers, Wotsits, breadsticks.

➢ Finger foods that don't dissolve: apple, cucumber, carrot. These offer more resistance and so greater biting pressure is required.

Sensory food exploration

These simple food exploration ideas have been adapted to be specifically suitable for babies and children with sight impairment.

Do all prep work ahead of time. Remember: To avoid sensory overload, introduce different taste, texture and activities one at a time. Try and use a range of tastes, to use all of the tongue, as babies do like variation. Food does not need to be bland and boring. Babies generally are more accepting of food if they see someone else eating it, but for a child with severe sight impairment you may have to make it more obvious, using some of the oral motor skills strategies below.

Note: Please do not introduce foods that are not developmentally suitable for your child, and beware of potential allergy or intolerances. Seek advice where necessary.

Activity 1: Sorting and stacking

Note: Your baby must be developmentally advanced enough to safely manipulate and chew small pieces of fruit or vegetables.

➤ Cut seasonal fruit into squares, so that baby can easily stack them.

➤ Use firmer fruit, like melon, pears and apples.

➤ Avoid overripe fruit.

➤ Accept that this will be messy! You can purchase extended bib tray kits that will help contain the food, or just use a plastic mat on the floor.

➤ Don't forget to lure her in by eating some of the fruit yourself. Try to choose something that will make an audible crunch.

Work together, and separately, to try to stack the fruit. Then progress to sorting the fruit by colour into an ice cube tray. If you are sorting, you can add irregular shapes like strawberry that have a really intense colour. As well as building awareness of food and textures, you are developing your baby's fine motor skills. The colours, textures, smells – and even your words describing the fruit – will stimulate her senses. Encourage curiosity and excitement as she explores with her hands and mouth. These descriptions are really important, as they explain to your child what she is discovering. Your role is to supply the information necessary for her to make sense of it all without vision.

Activity 2: Exploring slippery foods

For this activity, identify some more slippery foods – like pasta, boiled eggs, mangoes and bananas. Sometimes little ones don't enjoy slippery/slimy textures, and babies without vision are likely to find this challenging. Let her explore them with her hands and smell the food. The smell of egg is quite strong and distinctive. Slowly build familiarity with these new textures and smells. If your child has some useful vision, consider using spinach pasta, which adds colour and contrast as well as a bit more texture and nutrition. Possible progression: Use baked beans, which require more dexterity and also have a distinctive smell.

Activity 3: Painting with purees

Finger painting is attractive to most infants. This idea originally came from Ella's Kitchen (www. ellaskitchen.co.uk/), although any baby food pouches will work. If you prefer, you can buy your own fill and squeeze refillable food pouches. Food pouch squeezers provide the perfect edible paint – many supermarkets provide own label products at a reasonable price or, again, you can make your own. Icing bags also work quite effectively. Put a few drops on the tray and let your baby start to touch and taste it.

Use flavours that will provide a colour contrast with the surface and (preferably) have a distinctive smell. Once you have her interest, try letting baby hold the pouches and show her how to squeeze. This, too, is a messy activity, but it's not a waste of food. You are introducing new colours, textures and tastes; you are encouraging tactile exploration; building hand and finger strength; and making your child receptive to a wider variety of tastes and textures.

Using food to learn about the world is not only stimulating, it's soothing. Think about your own sensory feedback from stroking the cat or flipping colour change sequins. Sensory play can often settle an irritable baby. Remember: Babies rely on their senses to organise what they are learning, and it may take time for the learning to sink in.

Try this if your baby is teething. Fill an ice cube mould with fruit purees, then freeze it. Pop out individual cubes and use them as teething soothers for your baby! Put treats in a mesh bag before giving them to very little ones to suck on.

4.02–4.04: CUTLERY

The guidance below will help you work through using a spoon and fork and introducing a knife. At the same time, try to develop the child's play to support these skills. For manipulation and slicing, see the playdough activities below, as they work well and tie in with developing imaginative play. Sand is also a great medium to develop these skills. If you do not have access to a sandpit, put sand in a storage tub or deep tray. Start off with sand play toys like a small trowel, rake and fork. Then gradually reduce implement size, using serving spoons, then tablespoons, and alternate between wet and dry sand to vary weight and resistance. Dry sand also pours beautifully from one vessel to another.

4.05–4.07: DRINKING VESSELS

There are literally hundreds of different drinking vessels on the market for babies and small children, so it is difficult to choose what is best for your child. However, it has been established that it is important for a child with vision impairment to progress onto solid food as the learning window opens. Allowing a child to continue prolonged bottle feeding jeopardises this progression, so choosing a good, early alternative is vital.

According to the NHS and NCT (www.nct.org.uk), babies can learn to drink water from a cup from around six months old (sitting independently is best). Dentists suggest parents choose an open cup, free-flow cup or beaker rather than a sippy cup with valves. Your child may well spill drinks initially, but it does mean you avoid transitioning through multiple drinking vessels. Sipping rather than sucking is deemed better for a child's teeth. When very small, your baby will allow you to hold the cup and gently tip the water into her mouth. However, it won't be long before she gains confidence and tries to grab the cup, which may – at least for a while – result in rather more spillage! However, bear in mind that even non-spill cups can be spilled by a determined toddler. To reduce the chance of spills, do not overfill the beaker, and put a plastic bib on your child.

Two handles are easier for your child to locate and grasp, and strong, well-saturated colours that contrast with the surface are easier to see. If your child is orally sensitive, she may struggle with larger volumes of water in her mouth – a free-flow lidded cup will still reduce the flow, but avoids the need to suck. The design of the Munchkin Miracle® 360° has a natural-feeling top with a spill reduction mechanism that reduces mess while promoting good oral development.

4.08: LOAD AND SPOON FROM ONE VESSEL TO ANOTHER

If your child has some useful vision, look for something for her to manipulate that provides good contrast with both the spoon and the containers. Porridge oats lie well on the spoon, and chocolate rice pops contrast well with light-coloured dishes.

Cutlery progression guidance

Spoon – first stage
➢ Child-sized spoons with easy-to-grip handles are best to begin with. Look for strong colour contrasts.

➢ The smaller the child, the smaller the cutlery. Look out for food pushers to start with. Then progress to something like the Doddl range or the Munchkin Scooper™ – both are designed for the palmar grip.

➢ Some spoon handles curve inwards. This reduces the amount of wrist movement required to get the spoon in the mouth, and makes them easier for young children.

➢ Spoons with flat, shallow bowls are easier to eat from, but deeper bowls help keep food secure.

➢ Children usually hold their spoon or fork in their palm with a palmar grip, for a few years at least. They then switch to a more mature tripod grip, which most adults use. Worry less about the grip than success in getting food successfully from plate to mouth!

➢ Placing Dycem® mat under the plate can give more stability and prevent slipping. It will also provide colour contrast if necessary. Alternatively, you may find a damp cloth useful, or a piece of non-slip matting from a pound store.

Doddl infant cutlery

When the child has mastered using a spoon, move on to using a fork to stab cut up pieces of food and a spoon for 'scooping' food that is difficult to stab with a fork (e.g. beans, peas).

When the child has mastered using a spoon and fork, try some of the following activities to prepare them for using a knife and fork together. For this skill, the child will require improved bilateral coordination (coordination of left and right sides). The following activities focus on encouraging this coordination.

Playdough feeding activities

➢ Use playdough with a knife and fork to practise with 'pretend' food. Produce various thicknesses of dough, to encourage being able to cut through varying thicknesses/textures of food. You can add material to the dough, such as grains, seeds and/or rice. To make it a more engaging activity, make your own playdough and add scents and colouring.

➢ Practise placing the knife and fork in the correct hands and talk through this aspect. Remember to talk about 'left' and 'right', as there may be some confusion, and knowing which hand is which is very useful for a variety of activities. If you say 'right', touch the right hand or shoulder gently; then do the same for the left side. The touch reinforces understanding, but don't worry if your child does not grasp it straight away. Children are often 7 or 8 before they've gained a clear understanding of right and left.

➢ Encourage pushing the fork in the dough first, then cutting with the knife. Try cutting large and small pieces.

➢ Now move onto food: bananas cut easily, but are slimy to the touch. Gradually build up resistance.

Other useful activities for bilateral coordination

➢ Lego® and construction toys.

➢ Model-making.

➢ Cooking.

➢ Bead-threading.

➢ Weaving.

➢ Using a dustpan and brush.

➢ Screwing and unscrewing jars.

➢ Playing two-handed percussion instruments.

Habilitation skills

· ·

When the child shows good bilateral coordination, you may wish to use training cutlery to assist her in holding the cutlery correctly.

If the youngster has difficulty grasping cutlery, look for styles with thick handles, or build up the handles with foam. Junior Caring Cutlery is often a good start, but many high-street sets are just as good.

The child should be prompted to put their index fingers in the 'dips' of the Caring Cutlery. They should use a 'stab and saw' motion: stabbing the food with the fork and sawing back and forth with the knife. While she is learning to stab and saw effectively, the child may need adult hand over hand assistance.

· ·

44

5.00: Movement

5.00	MOVEMENT: UP AND MOVING – PROGRESSING TO MOVING FROM PLACE TO PLACE
5.01	Tummy time
	Gross motor and balance
5.02	Lift head and support
5.03	Push up from prone
5.04	Tuck legs/feet under
5.05	Bridge
5.06	Crawl
5.07	Respond or move towards sound
5.08	Pull to standing
5.09	Cruise furniture
5.10	Stand
5.11	Take steps
5.12	Stable gait, wide base
5.13	Good posture
5.14	Mature gait/walking
5.15	Climb
5.16	Upstairs crawling
5.17	Upstairs walking
5.18	Downstairs on bottom
5.19	Downstairs walking
5.20	Running
5.21	Jumping
5.22	Kick large ball
5.23	Throw
5.24	Catch sympathetically thrown object
5.25	Fine motor skills

Now that your child is moving, it is time to childproof your house!

Activities to work on these skills

Busy Bag: 12 Learn to skip

Handouts

8 10 simple ways to work on balance skills, 9 Stomp and catch/joey jump, 10 Row, Row, Row Your Boat, 11 Wake and Wiggle! Movement programme assessment, 12 Early directional concepts

Useful websites

➤ Primitive reflexes: youtu.be/vdiCep6OStA

➤ Pathways child development and tummy time: https://pathways.org/

https://pathways.org/topics-of-development/tummy-time/

➤ Sticky Kids, music and movement resources: www.stickykidscatalogue.co.uk/

www.youtube.com/channel/UC4u3fUr5gb7MrMLzj6jJ2UA

➤ Smart Moves motor skills movement programme: www.smartcc.co.uk/smart-smartmoves.html

5.01–5.06: THE IMPORTANCE OF TUMMY TIME

Movement begins even before birth and skills are developed through reflexes. These reflexes assist with the birthing process, support survival and provide rudimentary training for developing voluntary skills and movement. These reflexes are inhibited by the brain as the skills develop. Examples of primitive reflexes include rooting and the startle reflex. There is a lovely video on YouTube demonstrating all the reflexes found in a newborn baby (see 'Useful websites' above).

In babies, development occurs from the head down. They make phenomenal progress in a very short space of time and quickly develop head control in the upright position. Prone (lying on her front) control is more difficult and the weight of her head pulls it down. She needs to develop her neck control further and start working on her shoulders so she can push herself up. Without this strength, she will not move onto rolling, sitting independently or crawling. Each phase of each milestone is sequential, which is how it is possible to predict what a child should be achieving.

This is where tummy time comes in. For some reason, babies with severe visual impairment tend to object to tummy time. However, do persevere, as she will get used to it, particularly if she perceives it as a time to engage with a caregiver. Get down to her level, with your face close to hers. Tuck a small roll, or rolled blanket, under her chest/armpits to help her reach the correct position, and allow her to move her head and arms. Tummy time develops neck, shoulder, back and core stability and prepares the way for the next developmental milestones. Take the opportunity to find a variety of positions – such as lying her across your arm or knee – that make her feel safe but still allow her to develop. Pathways (https://pathways.org/) produce a phenomenal range of activities and leaflets to support your child's development. These are free to access and download and share, so long as you credit Pathways. The tummy time section explains the value of tummy time and offers a variety of ways to engage your baby. https://pathways.org/topics-of-development/tummy-time/.

She may need help to get her knees up and under, so she can start to lift up, create a bridge and prepare for crawling. This will then develop leg strength. You may need to provide something firm for her to push against, and also make sure that the surface she is on won't slip away.

Babies do still need to lie on their backs to develop different muscles and gain a different perspective. However, if she is a young baby (even if she has useful vision), nothing will fall within her focal range and initially even activity gyms will be out of reach.

Crawling is vitally important, developmentally speaking. It develops better coordination, gives more time to the development of core stability and promotes crossing the midline (an imaginary vertical line down the centre of the body which arms and legs need to cross to develop coordination and bilateral integration, as well as coordinating both sides of the brain). Your child is more likely to explore if she is well stimulated, understands that there are interesting things out there to find and feels secure. Make sure she becomes familiar with a small area where she can become confident moving round.

5.07: RESPOND OR MOVE TOWARDS SOUND

It can be difficult getting a baby with very low vision up and moving. Sometimes – without seeing all the things of interest around the room or watching what you are doing – he lacks motivation. Spending time on all the tummy time activities will help, because without a strong core and neck and shoulder strength he will not be able to lift himself into an effective crawling position.

Start with your voice, then introduce gentle toy sounds. Remember: A baby's hearing is delicate, so nothing too loud or strident, please.

Once he seems ready, use toys to stimulate his interest and then place them just within reach, but requiring a stretch. If he has a dominant hand, put the toys to the other side, so he'll have to reach across his body to get it. You are showing him that a little effort brings reward. Then try toys that will either rock or move away from him. Again, place them just within reach and, if he has some useful vision, make sure that they are brightly coloured as well as generate a sound.

There are many toys useful for this stage.

Little Tikes' Ocean Explorer Catch Me Crabbie has a motion sensor that makes it move from left to right in response to baby's movement, snapping its claws and playing music. Toys like the Bumble Ball (which create vibrations as well as audible feedback) are great for use with **resonance boards**. While the original Bumble Ball is no longer available, many derivatives are. To encourage crawling, look for toys like the VTech Crawl & Learn Bright Lights ball, with music and animal sounds and a built-in motor.

5.08–5.14: PULL TO STANDING TO MATURE GAIT

Getting going can be quite difficult, so once baby is up on all fours you can try rocking her backwards and forwards gently. As her balance tips, she should move her arm forwards to restore balance, and this is where the first elements of crawling start to emerge. In order to crawl, she must be able to support her weight through one arm as she reaches forward with the other one. This requires considerable upper body strength and balance, which will take time to achieve. The back and stomach muscles must also be well developed in order to stop her from sagging in the middle or dropping back to the floor. Static balance is easier to achieve than dynamic balance. Balance is static when sitting or standing still and it is easier to maintain than dynamic balance. When trying to move forwards or backwards, balance is dynamic. The movement means that the centre of balance changes all the time, so it is much more difficult to maintain.

Some babies bottom-shuffle and, while it is a normal part of development, it can be indicative of a baby who has not spent much time playing on their stomach and who may lack stability and strength. Such babies are often late walkers. They often have little motivation to walk, as they can shuffle round rapidly and feel more secure close to the floor.

Encourage her to pull herself onto her knees, against you or using a piece of furniture. Use a favourite musical toy or even a snack as a lure. Kneeling will help develop stability in the hips and lower body. Once you have this established, try encouraging her to pull to standing. Kneel on the floor in front of a low chair or sofa. Sit her on your knee, facing the sofa, with her feet flat on the floor and her knees and hips at 90 degrees. Use something to lure her to reach out and stretch and, as she does, holding her solidly round the hips, move her hips up and forwards to line up over her feet. Her knees should now be straight and she can lean forward and support herself against the sofa. Keep hold of her hips while she is developing her strength and stability. Give her plenty of praise and make sure she feels her efforts are rewarded.

5.15–5.19: CLIMBING, STEPS AND STAIRS

If you have a baby explorer on your hands, buy a stair gate! Actually, buy a stair gate anyway, as stairs are dangerous for young children – particularly those with vision impairment. However, you still need to allow her to learn how to tackle stairs, but only with your support.

Remember: Without vision, she will not be able to see the drop and won't understand the risk of falling.

Once she is crawling, she will happily use the same technique up the stairs. Climbing up is always easier than coming down, so concentrate on that first. You will probably need to teach a safe technique for descending. If she has a severe sight impairment, to start with don't introduce the idea of walking up and down the stairs, as crawling is safer. Coming down, show her how to sit on the step and 'bump' down each step. From the stairs below her, tug her leg to find the step below, and once she has secure contact bump her down one step. This is effective, but much safer than trying to walk down. Turn it into a game and emphasise the 'Bump!'

Once she progresses to walking up and down the stairs, don't hurry her. Her short legs make it difficult to negotiate stairs, so it is safer and easier to step down and bring the other foot onto the same step. Alternating feet onto steps is very complex and is likely to develop much later, so may need intervention. It is difficult to comprehend the process without actually seeing how others travel up and down the stairs.

Always encourage your child to hold the rail – particularly when descending – and keep your stairs free from clutter. Toddlers have a relatively large head and short arms and legs. At birth, the head makes up 25 per cent of a baby's length and the brain is about 25 per cent of its adult weight. However, by the age of 2, the brain has risen to 75 per cent of its adult weight, which means a toddler's head is disproportionately heavy. If the child tips forwards, the head's weight makes loss of balance more likely and it is difficult for an emergent walker to recover. Concentrate on building confidence going upstairs first: if she does fall, she will go forwards onto stairs, rather than out (and down) into space.

Gross motor skills

In early childhood there is no difference in the requirements or achievements of boys and girls. By the age of 3, a child should have gained all the basic gross motor movement skills he will require, but will continue to develop and refine them, yet without intervention children with severe vision impairment (SVI) will drop below the normal developmental timelines. If your child missed some developmental stages, progression can stall. However, all is not lost, because you can revisit skills, but just present them in an age and stage appropriate way. Occasionally a child may retain reflexes that should have been inhibited by the brain, and this too can cause developmental problems. Retained reflexes can sometimes be confused with other conditions, so it is worth seeking specialist advice.

If your child missed out the crawling stage, for instance, it can be worth going back and introducing games that require that skill. Crawling through tunnels and tents makes a great game. If your child doesn't understand crawling, or how to adopt the position, sit him on your lap, put your arm across his front and move him forward into a kneeling position, put his arms down and you have a starting position. This then allows you to move each of his feet forward to support a crawling movement.

Remember: Both boys and girls benefit from rough and tumble play. It develops body and spatial awareness, and particularly develops the vestibular system, as well as makes them more adventurous.

Some gross motor skills are very difficult to describe to a young child with SVI. Running is not walking fast – it requires the feet to be entirely unsupported, off the ground, for a short period of time. Skipping along, not over a rope, requires a combination of rhythmic stepping and hopping. These are both difficult concepts to grasp without vision.

5.20–5.21: RUNNING AND JUMPING

'Walking has often been defined as the process of continually losing and regaining balance whilst moving forward in an upright position' (Gallahue and Ozmun). No wonder, then, that a child with SVI finds it difficult. While, on average, a sighted child will be walking at around 12 months, there is a wide window, and neither 9 months nor 15 months is deemed exceptional. The biggest issue is the unnatural competition parents foist upon one another as they battle for their child to achieve certain milestones before others'. Some milestones, like walking, are given a disproportionate importance when comparing child development. Actually, it is crawling that is really significant in terms of development – building strength and coordination, as well as a mode of propulsion. In the same way, parents rush to buy their emergent walker new shoes, not realising that walking and stability progress better in bare feet. Children need to work through all the developmental stages at their own pace.

For small children, movement is often an uncoordinated mix between walking and running. Controlled jumping does not tend to come in before the age of three. For children with a vision impairment, it is very much a step into the unknown, so introduce jumping off very shallow steps, supporting the child with both hands or with gentle bouncing.

If your child struggles with stability and balance, or persists with a wide leg ('nappy') gait, please seek specialist advice. If there is no medical reason for the difficulty, undertake a movement assessment and draw up a programme of work for him (see Handout 11, Wake and Wiggle!, pages 189–199). Alternatively, purchase one of the many commercial movement programme packages (see the Useful websites section at the start of the chapter).

5.22: KICKING

Kicking requires the child to be able to balance on one leg and move the other leg with some force. It's a difficult thing to describe to a child with SVI.

Use a bell ball and roll it against your child's foot to spark his interest. Choose a lightweight ball that is large enough to increase the chances of successful contact. Praise every attempt, regardless of how successful he is. To maximise success, the ball must be rolled accurately and sympathetically to his feet. Initially, you may need to hold his hand initially for support.

Try walking forwards together rolling the ball in front of you, as each collision with the ball will prompt him to knock it away. You may need to work with your child on listening skills, so he becomes more aware of the ball's location. Once he can pick up where the ball is and has emergent kicking skills, you can start to become more adventurous with both speed and direction.

5.23–5.24: THROWING AND CATCHING

You will probably have to show your child how to lace her hands ready to receive whatever you throw. Before starting, practise with your child how to throw sympathetically. You want the toy to land gently and accurately in her outstretched hands, so that each attempt at catching is successful. It's a good idea to start with something small and light that will 'die' in her hands

(that is, does not bounce), so beanbags or Koosh balls are good. You can buy beanbags relatively cheaply, but can also make them yourself using a small piece of fabric and beans or rice. Alternatively, fill an old glove with dried beans and sew up the top. Do make sure there are no holes in the glove! The fingers make it easier to grasp the glove if the catch is just off centre.

As you progress, move onto larger items. Continue to avoid shiny, slippery balls, and look for things that are easier to grip. You can slow the travel of the ball by using Slo-Mo Balls™ or balloons, as these give your child more time to react. You may have to look for Slo-Mo Balls™ in specialist stores, but there are a number of commercially available balloon covers that make balloons safer for young children and reduce the risk of bursting – look for BubaBloon or Tumble Tots balloon covers, or the original Balzac. These all cover the balloon to make it more durable, reduce the risk of choking, and the material makes them easier to grip, but without adversely affecting the balloon's flight. Add rice inside the balloon to create sounds. You could also use inflated beach balls, but these are more difficult to grip and often rather large for small hands. As you progress to larger balls, get your child to hold her hands further apart and clap them together to catch.

Although your child has the ability to throw his dinner across the room from a very early age, controlled throwing comes later. This tends to develop as a result of understanding the reciprocal nature of throwing and catching.

Gross motor activities and games to try

➤ 10 simple ways to work on balance (Handout 8, pages 183–184).

➤ Animal walks – choose different animals and move round the room. Try an elephant with his trunk waving, a frog leaping around a room, a cat stretching and leaping or a snake slithering across the floor.

➤ Helping around the house – carry clothing to the washing machine, help load and unload the machine or even hand you clothes to hang on the line.

➤ Wake and Wiggle! (Handout 11, pages 189–199).

➤ Trampoline.

➤ Cycling.

➤ Hopscotch.

➤ Tig (also called tag).

➤ Playskool Poppin' Park Elefun® Busy Ball Popper®.

5.25: FINE MOTOR SKILLS

Fine motor skills do not develop in isolation. Baby development works from the head down and radiates outwards and, for good fine motor skills, gross motor skills first need to develop and be secure. Movement programmes such as Wake and Wiggle! (see Handout 11, pages 189–199) address gross motor skills that may have been missed or poorly developed, and help to improve concentration, balance, coordination and fine motor skills. To learn more about the theory behind this, read Sally Goddard Blythe's *The Well Balanced Child* (see References).

Why do we need to develop fine motor skills? Because they make dressing and undressing feasible, allow your child to finger feed and move onto wielding cutlery, and generally to become more independent. Areas to work on are:

➢ **Dexterity.**

➢ Grasping skills.

➢ Bilateral coordination.

➢ Hand and finger strength.

➢ Finger position and finger isolation.

➢ **Proprioception.**

Manual dexterity is the result of the development of gross motor skills, then fine motor skills, and progresses through the palmar, pincher and tripod grips. Bilateral coordination (the skill to move something from one hand to the other) develops concurrently, and for it to develop properly the hands must consistently cross the midline of the body. All these skills facilitate daily living tasks such as dressing and undressing, checking money, calculating change, drawing and writing, opening bottles or packaging.

Fine motor activities and games to try

➢ Shape sorter play – colours, shapes and dexterity.

➢ Dough disco (see below).

➢ Playdough play.

➢ Messy play in sand, cornflour, etc., that offers resistance (Busy Bag 14, Messy play, page 130).

➢ Using construction toys; Mega Bloks®, K'Nex®, Popoids, Duplo™, Lego™. The smaller the block, the greater skill level required.

> Building towers.

> Coins into a money box.

> Scribbling/drawing – aim to move from palmar to pincer grip, and finally a secure tripod grip.

> Putting clothes pegs along an edge.

> Using scissors – maybe start with sprung scissors.

> Threading beads or buttons.

> Sorting – see 'Make your own sorting tray' in the Introduction (pages xxx–xxx).

> Lacing.

> Popping bubble wrap (a great sensory activity, as physical pressure is rewarded by a pop that is both auditory and tactile).

> Finger puppet storytelling.

> Action and nursery rhymes (see Activity 1, pages 207–217).

If your child struggles with the pincer grip, try cutting the thumb and index finger off an old glove and get her to wear it. This will help her remember which fingers to use. The younger and less mature the child is, and the lower her vison, the more support she will need with each skill. All activities are stage, rather than age, appropriate.

These skills need to be in place for a child to be able to wield cutlery appropriately. Sand and messy play (with variable resistance) builds up the necessary skills for moving from finger feeding to good cutlery use.

Games to develop fine motor skills include:

> KerPlunk.

> Crocodile Dentist.

> Pop-Up Pirate!

> Buckaroo!

Dough disco

As a start, try these fun dough disco activities to develop fine motor skills (https://youtu.be/i-IfzeG1aC4), then build your own. Combining the activities with music makes them more memorable as well as being fun. Make playdough together to make it an all-round sensory experience (see the recipe in Handout 2, pages 174–175).

Using scissors

Scissors can be hard for severely sight impaired children. Without vision to see and model the action, understanding such a complex movement is difficult. There are many different types of scissors to consider – perhaps borrow some before you invest in a pair. All the scissors in the photograph are reasonably priced and readily available (form top to bottom: left-handed safety scissors, mother and child dual-control training scissors, right-handed safety scissors, easy grip squeeze scissors).

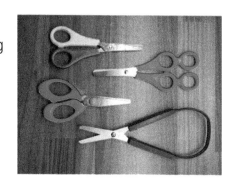

Consider whether your child can manipulate loop scissors or would be better starting with sprung scissors. Spending some time using the dual-control scissors may also convey the idea of what you are trying to achieve – more clearly than just a verbal description. Once you move onto more standard scissors, ask yourself if your child is left- or right-handed, as this makes a difference to the cutting edge. If she needs more support with motor skills or adaptations, get a referral to an **occupational therapist**.

The paper your child cuts should be neither too flimsy (making it difficult to control) nor too thick (your child has to exert too much force to succeed). If she has a preference for certain colours, choose them. Offer thin strips of paper that need only a single snip to cut the paper in half. Also, make sure the background contrasts, so your child can see there are now two pieces of paper. Increase the width of the paper gradually, so that two snips, and then three, are needed to cut the paper.

Draw thick dark straight lines, or use the sheets in Activity Sheet 5a (Using scissors, page 141), to see if your child can cut along them. If this does not work, you may have to use **Wikki Stix®** or raised tactile material to give her the line. Swell Paper works (if you can access it), because it creates a raised tactile line. However, it is expensive and requires specialist equipment. Making the Chinese lantern in Activity Sheet 5e (pages 145–146) is a good progression activity.

Then move onto adding bends and wiggles. Gradually increase complexity: use two-dimensional mathematical shapes (see below) to add another level of learning to the activity. Progress to making paper doll chains, snowflakes, etc. (www.auntannie.com/FridayFun/DollChain/).

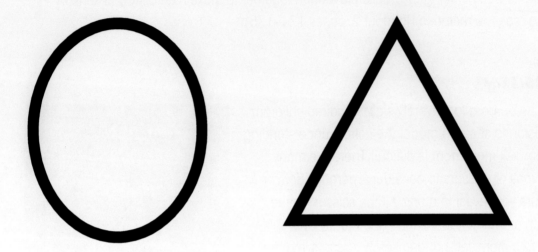

6.00: Early concept development

6.00	EARLY CONCEPT DEVELOPMENT
6.01	Demonstrate understanding of object permanence
6.02	Respond to/show preference for different textures
6.03	Cause and effect, e.g. press button on toy to get reaction
6.04	Simple direction concepts: up/down, etc.
6.05	Recognition of different shapes/textures
	Early time
6.06	Day/night
6.07	Light/dark
6.08	Seasons
6.09	Days
6.10	Recognition of money from other objects
6.11	Understanding handing over money to buy goods
	Body awareness
6.12	Body parts on self
6.13	Body parts on others
6.14	Active nursery rhyme participation
	Understanding simple instructions
6.15	Respond to own name
6.16	Respond to '**Stop**'
6.17	One instruction
6.18	Two instructions
6.19	Take message

Activities to work on these skills

Busy Bags: 5 Treasure baskets, 7 Mobility adventure walk, 14 Messy play

Activity Sheets: 7 1p sum sheet, 8 2p sum sheet, 11 My first body parts, 13 Sensory scavenger hunt

Activity: 1 Songs and rhymes

Progression: Busy Bag 9 The money game, Activity Sheet 9 Coin identification, Activity Sheet 10 Clock face

To work on prerequisite skills

Refer back to discussion of body awareness, body parts, finger separation and manual dexterity – fine motor development in the Introduction (pages 7–13).

Busy Bag: 6 Bath paint

Handouts

12 Early directional concepts, Online resource 2 Concepts and manipulation, 3 Concepts and opposites

13 First body parts, Online resource 1 Body parts

Useful website

➢ Coins game: www.topmarks.co.uk/money/coins-game

6.01: OBJECT PERMANENCE

The term **object permanence** was coined by child psychologist **Jean Piaget** and signifies the start of the differentiation of self from the rest of the world. It is the understanding that objects continue to exist even when they cannot be perceived (this includes all the senses, so the object cannot be seen, heard, felt, smelled or sensed in any way).

Babies usually start to understand object permanence from around 6 months of age. The process continues to be refined up to the age of 2. However, for babies with a vision impairment, onset can be much later and averages at around 15 months.

Infants tend to develop the idea of 'mother permanence' before object permanence, which is aided by the fact that the mother figure returns. Initially, babies identify mothers by smell and touch more than vision. Remember: For the severely vision impaired infant, most contact with objects is accidental, and with subsequent contact it can be difficult for the child to be certain that it is the same object.

Object permanence will help your child understand the world around him. It will help him anticipate what will come next, build his understanding of self and others and make him more confident and secure in relationships.

Activities to build object permanence

➤ Peekaboo – most children have got some vision, so make the most of it. Don't hide behind your hands, but use a brightly coloured cloth to hide behind. Use an interesting texture for additional stimulation (after all, you want your child to look for you!).

➤ Leave the room – however, to make sure out of sight is not out of mind, keep talking to him. Gradually reduce how much you say, and reduce the volume.

➤ Sensory tubs – bury small toys or other objects in a tub of rice (or flour, oats…) something similar. Try to include a variety of shapes and textures.

6.02: TEXTURES

Introduce a variety of textures from very early on. Many toys are plastic and, while entertaining and educational, they all feel the same in terms of texture. Remember: Younger babies tend to explore everything with their mouths, so supervise your child closely when introducing textures, and avoid things that could be dangerous. Natural textures are a good starting point in a treasure basket. Wooden spoons, pine cones, soft smooth ribbon, felt, sponge, a piece of loofah – these are all great textures to explore. Scrunchy paper is also good to include, particularly if it has a holographic pattern that catches the light. Keep the contents of the treasure basket the same for a while, so your child becomes familiar with the textures. You can then add something different and eventually move onto baskets themed around a particular topic or colour.

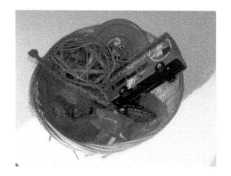

Some children dislike certain textures and some display **sensory avoidance** of them. This used to be called tactile defensiveness, but it is now recognised as being a broader issue. Vision is the dominant sense, integrating the senses so they work together seamlessly. However, without vision, **sensory integration** can be a problem. Some children may be sensory seekers, while others may be sensory avoidant. This may be as a result of hypersensitivity, which the child finds overwhelming.

Messy play is a great way to introduce a variety of textures and reduce hypersensitivity. See Busy Bag 14 (Messy play, page 130). Also look for books that include textures, such as the *That's not my…* or the *Never Touch a…* series (Usborne Publishing and Make Believe Books, respectively).

6.03: CAUSE AND EFFECT

For older children, cause and effect is about understanding why things happen and making predictions. For small children, it is more about action and reaction and instant gratification. However, if a child does not understand that if he presses the button the music will play, he won't develop more complex reasoning and predictive skills. He needs to understand that there is a direct connection between his actions and the world around him. But, without useful vision and the ability to see the results of actions, this realisation can be slower to develop. Think about the way a sighted child heads for the remote control at every opportunity – the toy one will not do, it has to be the real thing! The baby has seen the magic that the remote control can create and nothing else will do. He starts to develop motivation to move (to get the remote, and explore) – to see if there is anything else out there equally entertaining.

A child with a vision impairment needs direct intervention to compensate for the lack of incidental learning. You can start encouraging and rewarding movement very early on.

Bathtime provides lots of opportunities to develop baby's understanding. The simple act of waving hands or feet is rewarded by splashing. Although some babies may be surprised by the splash, persevere, as it also helps build an understanding of texture, and other concepts such as action and consequence and anticipation.

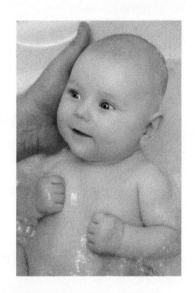

Put ankle or wrist bells on baby, so that movement is rewarded.

Lie her on her back in an activity gym where the toys are easily within reach, should she lift her hands. You can extend this idea later by creating an arch of safe household items or by building a **Little Room** playcentre (find more information about Little Rooms at www.lilliworks.org). Remember: At this stage, exploration is often accidental and needs to be encouraged.

Once she can sit up well, seated activity centres are good, because they don't require a refined touch to elicit an audible response. Choose one with a variety of textures and sounds – you may need to demonstrate the activities that are not immediately in front of your child, because with low vision she may not realise they are there. Don't be tempted to use a sit-in baby walker instead. They do not assist with walking, but help infants to reach things that are beyond their understanding and/or dangerous. It is all too easy for a baby walker to tip over due to even a small change in terrain, including toys on the floor. A suitable supportive alternative might be a Bumbo floor seat. These provide back support, along with more secure sitting, and can accommodate a tray.

As she progresses, draw her attention to cause and effect. Press keys on a piano together or play with electronic toys. Always do this together, to ensure she gets the positive response she needs to develop her understanding.

6.04: DIRECTIONAL CONCEPTS

Talk to your child about movement and direction from a very early age. When you lift him up, emphasise 'Up'. When you put him down, say 'Down' clearly, spin him 'Round' and describe what's happening. Even when he is still in a buggy, you can point out that you are going forwards, when you are going up the hill and when you are going down. Tell him you are turning left and right, because – even if he doesn't understand the exact word – you are building his understanding. He will need to understand directional concepts and terminology if he is going to become an independent traveller. Use Handout 12 (Early directional concepts, page 200) or Online Resources 2 and 4 (Concepts and manipulation and Directional concepts) to remind you of the main directional concepts and terms. Use them accurately, in context, regularly.

6.05: SHAPE AND TEXTURE

Early play experiences introduce shape and texture, but for children with SVI the teaching needs to be more detailed and prolonged. There are a variety of shape sorters on the market that can introduce and reinforce shape and texture. If possible, find alternatives to plastic, because – even though the surface texture can be varied – the feel of plastic remains the same. Initially, when sorting by touch alone, the name of the shape is by the by, but the use of correct terminology is important once the shape is identified. A circle is two-dimensional, a sphere is three-dimensional (but so is a ball), and that may be easier to understand initially. Some three-dimensional shapes are very complex and don't need exploring in detail at this stage.

When considering shape and texture introduce 'WESST' when exploring an object – determining its Weight, Edges, Size, Shape (Smell) and Texture. If applied consistently, this systematic approach provides greater understanding of objects, shape and texture.

6.06–6.09: EARLY TIME

The passage of time covers many things (day and night, seasons, days of the week, months of the year), and is addressed before telling the time. Telling the time is complex and often comes late to children with learning difficulties. However, seasonal change is more easily absorbed.

Introduce your child to each season as you encounter it.

➤ **Spring** brings new growth, early blossom and a reawakening. Plant bulbs for spring flowering or look for snowdrops.

➢ **Summer** offers warmth, long grass and daisies on the lawn. There is an abundance of flowers and intriguing smells, combined with more audible insects, birds and wildlife.

➢ **Autumn** brings fruits and harvest festivals, and the leaves start to fall. Scuffing through leaves is great fun and brings home the nature of the season. Gather leaves, conkers and pine cones for a seasonal treasure basket.

➢ **Winter** brings frost and snow – markedly different from the rest of the year. If the weather is not extreme enough, look for indoor snow play centres near where you live.

Use seasonal outings to explain what clothes are suited to which weather. You can reinforce this by getting your child to select weather appropriate clothing for their doll or teddy.

Your child then needs to comprehend the difference between weekdays and weekends. Monday to Friday, you go to school or work. Practise reciting the days of the week, or look online for rhymes that help embed learning. Things like 'Solomon Grundy' work well, but are very dated now.

Months of the year

Thirty days hath September,
April, June and November:
All the rest have thirty-one,
Saving February alone
And that has twenty-eight days clear,
And twenty-nine in each leap year.

Try to get your child familiar with the analogue clock face. It's all too easy to ignore it (with the prevalence of talking and digital time pieces), but the clock face brings a different understanding of time and provides directional concepts that can be used for turning or locating food on a plate. Learn the numbers as they appear on a clock, and the layout. There are some good clock face shape sorters on the market. If your child has an aptitude, you can progress to looking at 'o'clock'. For directional purposes, 3, 6, 9 and 12 are the most significant. See Activity Sheet 10 (Clock face, pages 154–155).

Distinguishing between day and night can prove a real problem to children with no useful vision. Sleep problems are not unusual, but there are a number of things you can do to avoid or alleviate these issues.

➢ Establish a clear bedtime routine and stick to it. It may need to change as he matures, but the principles should be constant. We all need cues to tell us it is bedtime, to prompt the release of melatonin and help us settle.

➢ Where possible, create a routine that encourages your child to self-settle. That way, if he wakes in the night he will know how to go back off to sleep.

➢ Sleep in the dark, as it helps the body release melatonin. Babies find it comforting and relaxing and too much exposure to bright light when put to bed can throw the body clock out of rhythm. Children's eyes let in more light than adults' eyes and exposure to bright light shuts down melatonin production. Remember: Many children with SVI have some useful vision, and most will see some light.

➢ With older children, beware of blue light emitted from electronic devices like tablets. These should be switched off at least half an hour before bed, or sleep can be adversely affected.

➢ If you put your child into a travel cot to play, make sure it's not the bed that you expect them to sleep in. This can send mixed messages and disrupt sleep patterns.

If your child struggles with sleep, you may find your community or health visiting team can advise. School nurses are also a good source of advice. If your child has an appropriate diagnosis, **Cerebra** may be able to help. They offer general advice and practical one-to-one support (https://cerebra.org.uk/get-advice-support/sleep-advice-service/).

6.10–6.11: EARLY MONEY

For children with a vision impairment, and particularly those with additional difficulties, there is often insufficient time in the National Curriculum for them to absorb adequate money handling skills. These skills often come late to children with learning difficulties. and it can be difficult to find appropriate ways of putting them in place for older pupils. Early money handling can prove extremely helpful and encourages a positive view of money skills – as a means to an end rather than a mathematical exercise. Strategies will need to vary, dependent on the age and ability of children, but here are a few basic suggestions.

Coin identification

Use real money every time. Don't be tempted to use plastic coins, as they simply won't feel the same. Remember: Tactile recognition includes weight and texture, not just shape.

➢ Introduce one or two coins first (1p and 2p coins are ideal).

➢ Work towards recognising money from other similar items.

➢ Progress to being able to identify individual coins.

➢ Gradually increase the range of coins used.

➢ Introduce the idea of money for purchasing.

➢ Any money handling is beneficial. Give your child small coins to save in a piggy bank.

➢ Look and feel the coins yourself.

The physical difference in size between 1p and 5p is minimal; the same applies to the 2p and the 10p. For ease, it can be easier to work just with 1p and 2p coins, rather than confuse the child. Visually, with SVI it can be difficult for a child to distinguish between copper and silver. Instead, run your fingernail along the edge of the coin: circular copper coins are smooth, silver coins have ridges. The 20p and 50p are distinctively different sizes, and have an easily distinguishable shape. However, if the child does not understand 'bigger' and 'smaller', confusion will occur. He needs to be able to correctly sort coins into denominations before being able to line them up in ascending or descending order. Confusion frequently arises over the discrepancy between coin sizes and their face value (for instance, a 2p is not worth more than a 20p just because it is bigger).

Invest in a plastic till and a small purse. Always encourage placing money in a purse or wallet, because it's best to make it a habit early on. You will have to find lots of different ways of working at the same level and still keeping hold of the child's interest. Create your own play shop. You can buy and sell anything for pennies.

Keep the pound coins separate, initially, to avoid confusion. Most small children mix up pennies and pounds anyway.

Take your child shopping. Encourage him to take part in the process.

Allow him to hand the money over for individual items and interact with shop assistants. In these circumstances, spending a pound coin in a pound shop provides a great simple activity. Although starting with pennies is advised, visiting a pound shop can be a useful experience, as purchasing one thing for £1 is such a simple idea to grasp. The value at this point doesn't matter, but a single coin handed over provides immediate reward and introduces the idea of what money is used for. Some pound shops have recently extended the range of products on sale, and introduced a wider range of pricing. This has somewhat clouded the issue, but this principle still works well in most pound shops.

Progression

Once your child can count single coins or add a couple on, try The money game (Busy Bag 9, pages 113–116). You will need two dice (preferably tactile), a large pile of 1p and 2p coins (you can progress to other coins later). Adjust the rules to suit, making the game as simple or complex as you wish by changing the coin values. You can have a set number of turns, or play until someone runs out of money, or just count up the coins in front of the players at the end.

6.12–6.14: BODY AWARENESS

Body awareness is one of the building blocks on which concept development is built. The conceptual understanding of the body in space and the environment gives purpose to movement. The greater the child's understanding of basic concepts, the greater the understanding of more abstract concepts and reasoning. However, without useful vision, body awareness and concepts must be taught specifically. Direct targeted intervention enhances body awareness and concept development and reduces developmental delay.

A child needs to know his own body shape, size and how it moves, as well as being able to identify each and every body part on himself and then on other people. It is part of the development of self. You don't learn it all at once, but build, layer upon layer. For instance, you might talk about arms and legs with a small child, but only add the concepts of shin or calf at a later date when the initial terminology is secure. You can support learning through play, using toys like Mr. Potato Head.

Baby massage is known to soothe a fractious child, but it is also wonderful for extending body awareness. Ensure you highlight joints and the way they move, as well as making sure you reach the very tips of fingers and toes. Separate each finger to indicate each separate digit, and perhaps combine with soothing songs or nursery rhymes. The rhymes in Appendix 4 (pages 207–217) will provide a starting point. There are also several worksheet checklists to evaluate and work on body awareness and concepts as your child progresses (Activity Sheet 11, Body parts, page 156; Online Resource 1, Body parts; Handouts 11 Wake and Wiggle! assessment, page 189, and Wake and Wiggle! Session 1, Body parts, page 194).

Bathtime with babies has already been discussed in this chapter (page 60), but older children still benefit from developing body awareness in the bath. Why not use Busy Bag 6 (Bath paint, pages 106–107) and use bath crayons (or bath paints) in the bath to draw on arms and legs? Alternatively, try changing the colour of the bath water, or even its consistency. You can buy a range of products to turn the bath water into jelly, goo, slime, or just a glitter bath. Search for Smelli Gelli Baff or Glitter Slime Baff, or Lush Fun soaps (which you can mould into different shapes).

6.15–6.19: FOLLOWING INSTRUCTIONS

Once your child develops a degree of independence, you will be able to change your descriptive language into instructions. Following instructions develops attention and listening skills – skills that your child will need in order to develop and keep herself safe as she progresses. You need her to be able to process and respond to your simple instructions, to direct her moving around and compensate for the lack of visual input. She should understand and respond to her name from the age of 6 or 7 months onwards, but may not be able to follow even a simple instruction before 18 months old or so. The more severe the vision impairment, the greater the delay in following instructions that require her to move. This is because of the number of complex skills she will need.

Give clear and specific instructions that are age appropriate and based on things that you and your child have done and talked about together. When you say 'Wave bye bye', even though you are moving her arm, this is technically an instruction. The more you rehearse it, the sooner she will understand she should wave when you give the instruction. Waving is an important salutation for your child to understand and use. Bear in mind that children with SVI need gesture to be taught.

Initially, she will only be able to follow one simple instruction at a time – for instance, 'Put your coat on.' Keep it clear and give her time to process your instruction. 'Go get your coat' is much more complex – it requires an understanding of object permanence, as well as locomotor, orientation and navigational skills. There is also an inference that she will go, get and bring the coat back that is not stated. Rehearse clear single instructions and build her repertoire, so that eventually you will be able to join two instructions together.

You will then be able to extend this to 'Go and get your coat and put it on.' If she seems reluctant, it may be that the request is too complex and is overloading her. Remember: There is only minimal challenge to a sighted child skipping off to get her coat, but for one with severe vision impairment this could be a huge task. The problem may not be comprehension, but the actual execution. There is no hurry: build competence at each level before progressing.

Progression from here will be to take a message and return with a response. However, before your child can undertake tasks alone without holding hands, she must reliably respond to her name and an instruction to 'Stop'. The likelihood is that your child will be in school before this is achieved, but maybe not, as each child is different and has their own strengths. In primary school, children are often sent to collect the register, often accompanied by an adult, but this still requires them to go somewhere, remember what they are asking for, then obtain and return with the register. It demands a great deal of concentration and attention to detail and listening skills, as well as memory skills and retention of information and interaction with someone else. This is no mean feat – at all!

7.00: Listening and looking

7.00	LISTENING AND LOOKING
7.01	Turn to sound
7.02	Identify voice
7.03	Auditory tracking of object or toy
7.04	Identify household sounds
7.05	Identify environmental sounds
7.06	Identify vehicle sounds
7.07	Extend understanding and use of sound
7.08	Visual tracking of object or toy
7.09	Reach for object
7.10	Primary colour recognition
7.11	Reach across midline to retrieve
7.12	Sort visually

Activities to work on these skills

Activity: 1 Songs and rhymes, 2 Create your own story bags

Progression

Busy Bag: 7 Mobility adventure walk

Activity Sheets: 12 Motor scavenger hunt, 13 Sensory scavenger hunt

Useful websites

➤ Scottish Sensory Centre 'Visually impairing conditions': www.ssc.education.ed.ac.uk/resources/vi&multi/eyeconds/list.html

➤ Daniel Kish video footage on the BBC: www.bbc.co.uk/news/av/magazine-3 www.bbc.co.uk/programmes/b0709v4m

➤ Information and support for deafblind or children with complex needs: www.sense.org.uk/

➤ Picture Exchange Communication System: https://pecs-unitedkingdom.com/pecs/.

Depending on who you consult, it is thought that between 80 and 90 per cent of information is presented visually. Younger children rely extensively on visual information, on watching what is going on around them and modelling activities. If their vision is good enough, they can check back to confirm what they saw. Think about all the visual displays and pictures in a foundation stage classroom. Listening is more transitory and requires more concentration. It takes longer to identify something by sound alone – and, once the child thinks he has identified it, it could be gone. Each spoken word disappears as soon as it is said.

A child with vision impairments needs to be taught how to listen and how to maximise her vision to support her understanding. If this is supported early, she will find school less overwhelming. Severely vision impaired (SVI) children are required to have ridiculously high concentration levels to learn in a sighted world, and it is very tiring.

If your child has a dual sensory impairment or complex needs, you may like to seek support from Sense (www.sense.org.uk). Some children may need to communicate using Makaton, BSL (British Sign Language), on-body signing, PECs (Picture Exchange Communication System) or by using the deafblind manual.

If the child uses BSL, be aware of her visual fields and make sure you sign in the area that she sees most clearly. Wear plain clothing that contrasts well with the colour of your hands, so she can see the shapes you are forming. If she lip-reads, again ensure your face is central in her field of vision. Good communication is vital to your child's development, so make sure you understand what she needs.

THE EAR AND DEVELOPMENT OF HEARING

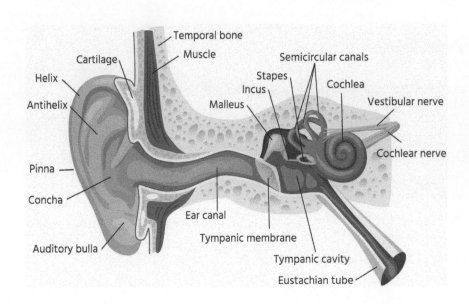

7.01–7.02: TURN TO SOUND AND IDENTIFY VOICE

A baby will identify and turn to her mother's voice at around 3 to 4 months of age. Recognising Mum's voice comes quite easily, because she has been listening to it in the womb for months, but she is less attuned to other people's voices. Newborn babies respond best to high-pitched and sing-song voices.

Encourage everyone to introduce themselves by name as a matter of course, unless they are very immediate family. It is frustrating and infuriating when people expect a child to know who they are, or (even worse) to have to guess. People still believe that those with vision impairments magically develop super-hearing. This is not the case – the development of listening skills requires considerable work. However, the child is able to use spare brain capacity to interpret sound in more detail and refine her listening skills.

Your child's hearing is sensitive at first and can be damaged by loud noise. She will start to follow other sounds with her eyes between 4 and 6 months and should start to notice toys that make a noise. This stage may be missing, or occur later, with SVI, which means that other stages will also be delayed. By age 3, she should have a word for everything and should recognise and respond to you from another room. Always tell her when you leave the room, and continue to talk, as this will encourage her to concentrate or may motivate her to follow you.

Verbal input should be clear and precise. Give her time to process what you have said – and if she doesn't respond, repeat what you said exactly. If you change the phrasing, it will require a whole new process. Only change your phrasing if you still haven't elicited a response after allowing processing time and repetition.

7.03: AUDITORY TRACKING OF OBJECT OR TOY

Use your child's play to develop her understanding and use of sound. Use toys that move and make noise, as this introduces auditory tracking. Initially, keep the toy close at hand to engage the child's interest, then gradually extend the range.

7.04: IDENTIFY HOUSEHOLD SOUNDS

When you move round the house, try to find places or rooms that echo. Bathrooms or other rooms with few or no soft furnishings give an audible echo. Once your child has sufficient vocabulary, play games moving round the house and getting her to identify the different rooms.

Play sound bingo. Identify all the different household noises by name. Babies seem to be attracted to the sound of the washing machine in particular, and many find it soothing. It broadens sound recognition and begins the process of developing attention to sound and concentration, even though this is fleeting at this point.

You can further develop echolocation by singing or chattering into a bucket and pointing out how different it sounds. If you want to find out more about the use of echolocation for navigation, investigate the works of Daniel Kish (https://www.abc.net.au/btn/classroom/bat-man/10533060, https://worldaccessfortheblind.net/facilitating-movement-and-navigation-blind-pre-schoolers-positive-practical-approach). He encourages using echolocation, which he calls Flash Sonar, for those with vision impairment. Not everyone can use it to this level, but it can be a very useful skill when combined with other skills and strategies.

Note: If your child sleeps in the day, do not reduce household noise. Your child will get used to low-level noise and may even find it reassuring.

7.05: IDENTIFY ENVIRONMENTAL SOUNDS

Don't let your child go out and about with her hood up, as this restricts her vision and makes it difficult to tell the which direction noise is coming from. A beanie or bobble hat that doesn't cover her ears will keep her head warm without impacting on vision or hearing.

If your child has a hearing impairment and has a radio aid, be aware that the noise can be overwhelming when she is outside. Traffic and wind noise can be particularly difficult to cope with, as they mask other sounds.

Children seem to love echoes, so make the most of anything that does so, as it hones listening skills. Build on the echoes you introduced in the bathroom (see previous section), and really go to town under tunnels and bridges, for instance. Stamp your feet, call 'Echooooooo', shout 'Hellooooooo', or sing if you are feeling really brave.

Once you have established that objects can change sound, you can develop echo and sound shadows (areas of muted or deadened sound) in more detail. Find a bus shelter and play with the echoes inside. Then try approaching the shelter, stamping your feet, to see if she can pick up the change in sound that indicates something is there. As well as echoing back, bus shelters create a sound shadow. As vehicles go past, you can hear them coming towards you, identify when they are alongside and as they move away. When there is something reasonably solid between you and the traffic, the traffic sound is muted.

7.06: IDENTIFY VEHICLE SOUNDS

Note: For more information about listening to traffic out and about, refer to 'Road safety' (pages 74–80).

Introduce a broad range of sounds in different situations and develop your child's concentration levels. All these skills will be used to increase her vocabulary and enhance her understanding of the world, and will eventually be used for navigation and orientation.

7.07: ACTIVITIES TO TRY TO EXTEND UNDERSTANDING AND USE OF SOUND

➢ When bathing, turn the tap on and off and get your child to tell you when the tap is running.

➢ Play hide-and-seek together, but looking for something audible.

➢ Sound bingo – make your own, or buy one like Galt Soundtracks.

➢ Make a string telephone. You will you need two large paper cups and a length of string. Make a very small hole in the base of the cup, just big enough for the string, and tie a knot to stop it pulling through. In order to work, the string needs to be taut.

➢ Sound games on an iPad or tablet.

The eye – development and stimulation of vision

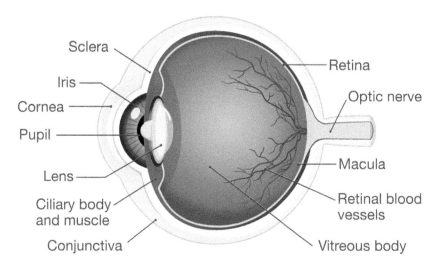

When a baby is born, vision is quite limited and she can only focus 20–30 cm (8–12 in) away, which is roughly the distance from her face to yours when she is feeding. Even if your child has a vision impairment from birth, there is much you can do to stimulate her vision and visual processing as she learns to use her vision over time.

With normal vision, she should start following moving objects from around 3 months, although with SVI this will be later. The eyes only start to work together properly somewhere between 5 and 8 months. Both eyes need to work together if your child is going to be able to use depth perception.

Depth perception helps you recognise the difference between a change of surface colour and a drop, like a step.

Different vision impairments affect different parts of the eye, so different aspects of vision are impaired (find out more about eye conditions on the Scottish Sensory Centre website, www.ssc.education. ed.ac.uk). Your QTVI or habilitation specialist will also be able to elaborate on the potential impact of certain eye conditions.

If your child has CVI (cortical vision impairment), it is more difficult to predict what she can see. CVI is caused by damage to the visual pathways in the brain, and children with the condition can see certain things (or in certain circumstances), but not in others. They really struggle when there is too much visual clutter.

A child with vision impairment will take longer to scan and locate an object and to process visual information. Whatever activities you undertake, allow your child extra processing time. Use items in well-saturated primary colours against a clear, uncluttered background. Gradually increase the range of colours, add more things and smaller items. Generally, good task lighting will help too, but it does depend on your child's eye condition.

If spectacles or glasses help your child, encourage her to wear them and make sure they are kept clean. If your child struggles with glare when she is out and about, she may benefit from prescription tinted glasses. Alternatively, a peaked hat or cap or a sunshield may help. Some children struggle with glare in bright conditions, and others struggle in low lighting at night, or even at dusk. Discuss the implications of your child's vision impairment with your child's ophthalmic consultant, QTVI or your habilitation specialist.

7.08–7.09 VISUAL TRACKING AND REACHING FOR OBJECT OR TOY

Sit your child on the floor with legs outstretched and roll the ball down her legs. This way, she has a tactile (as well as visual) stimulus to draw her attention. You can progress to trapping the ball between her legs, so that it is free rolling but contained within a narrow space. This is an effective alternative to noisy toys, which serve a similar purpose. If your child is attracted by toy vehicles, look for something like the VTech Toot-Toot range, which offers lots of interaction as the vehicle moves along.

Once scanning and tracking is going well, try placing the toy to one side and encouraging your child to reach across her midline for the toy. This extends the range that she is scanning over, and also improves coordination and balance. To initiate scanning and tracking, always use items that your child finds attractive. There are many different versions of the light ball available, and these always attract children.

7.08–7.12: ACTIVITIES TO DEVELOP LOOKING, REACHING AND SORTING

➢ Sort buttons or toys visually or make patterns using pegs.

➢ Match toys of similar colours.

➢ Play with toys using a magnifying glass to allow her to see more detail, or take a magnifying bug pot on the Sensory scavenger hunt (Activity Sheet 13, pages 160–161).

➢ Play skittles – but remember to contrast the ball and skittles and skittles and floor.

➢ Make a toilet roll telescope – this changes the way the child sees things.

➢ Be pirates! An eyepatch completely changes what the child sees and encourages development in the uncovered eye. Add a telescope, and you have a perfect costume.

➢ Hang up real items, like utensils, so the child can see from different angles.

➢ Sit on floor, and contain a ball or car with her legs. Try similar activities that work from side to side, and towards and away.

➢ Try scanning and tracking up and down. Once you have the child engaged, toss a bright ball in the air. Try using balloons, as they move slower than balls.

➢ Chase bubbles.

➢ With an electronic device, such as an iPad, for visual tracking and listening, use apps like Sensory Sound Box, Sensory Light Box or Tap-n-See.

If your child is struggling with these activities, try attracting her attention with a puppet. You can have the puppet close up and make sure it falls within her field of vision. Play 'Peep-bo' (or 'Peekaboo') with the puppet. Alternatively, try using finger puppets really close to her face and re-enact familiar fairy stories. Then get her to join in, using some characters on each hand, so she is using both hands together.

8.00: Road safety

8.00	EARLY ROAD SAFETY AWARENESS
8.01	Pavements are for people, roads are for vehicles
8.02	Hold hands
8.03	Name main vehicle types, e.g. bus, lorry
8.04	Safer places to cross
8.05	Push button on pelican
8.06	Early environmental awareness, textures, gradients

Activities to work on these skills

Busy Bag: 7 Mobility adventure walk

Activity Sheet: 14 Post a letter

Progression

Activity Sheet: 16 Urban trail

Prerequisite skills

Understanding and responding to instructions, including 'Stop' (see 6.00, 'Early concepts', pages 57–66)

Activity Sheets: 12 Motor scavenger hunt, 13 Sensory scavenger hunt

Handout

14 Stop look and listen

Useful websites

➢ RoSPA car seat advice: www.childcarseats.org.uk/choosing-using/

➢ Road safety: www.think.gov.uk/education-resources/

➢ Road Safety Scotland: https://roadsafety.scot/

➢ Beep Beep! Days: https://brakezebras.org/beep

➢ Road safety week: www.roadsafetyweek.org.uk/

➢ Road safety Northern Ireland: www.nidirect.gov.uk/articles/road-safety-children-under-seven

➢ Dog, Duck & Cat Trust: www.dogduckandcat.co.uk/

➢ Go Safe with Ziggy: https://roadsafety.scot/learning/early/go-safe-with-ziggy/

A baby's first experience of road safety is often the journey home from the hospital, safely ensconced in their first-size car seat.

In the UK, babies and children under the age of 12, or 135 cm (53 in) tall, are required by law to use age appropriate car seats. For small babies, this means a rear-facing seat, preferably in the back of the vehicle. It is mandatory for all children to be carried rearward facing until at least 15 months old (seat sizes 0 and 0+; up to 83cm). According to the Royal Society for the Prevention of Accidents (RoSPA), it has been shown that children in rear-facing seats are up to five times safer than those in forward-facing ones. RoSPA produces extensive guidance on choosing and fitting appropriate car seats.

Even if you don't have your own car, you probably still travel in one from time to time. A rear-facing seat can be quite disconcerting for a baby with a severe vision impairment, as all he can see is the back of the seat. If he has some useful vision, you may like to invest in a two-way mirror – this allows you to see him, and him to see you.

Remember: The distances involved may make it difficult for him to see you. You may prefer to install his seat in the front, where he is closer to you, but don't forget to deactivate any airbags.

Try and keep him occupied in the vehicle. For rear-facing babies, there is a lovely range of kick toys that fasten onto the back of the seat. Look for Taf Toys' Play and Kick Car Toy. available from most major retailers. Once he is older and able to sit in a forward-facing seat, make sure that any toys are secured, and interact with him so he does not feel alone. Playing songs or rhymes may also keep him entertained if you are concentrating on driving.

Once he becomes more dextrous and figures out how to undo his seatbelt, he will! It's a phase that many children go through, and most grow out of, but one that needs consistent and firm handling. First, make sure he understands that everyone has to be fastened in. A search online produces a number of songs and rhymes you can sing as each passenger gets fastened in. This makes the process more memorable and reinforces the fact that it applies to everyone. Do not start your engine until everyone is fastened in and, if he does undo his belt, pull in and stop until he is fastened in again. Turn the engine off, so he knows the car is stopped. This has the most impact if he knows he is going somewhere especially nice. There are some simple stories and activities on the **Dog, Duck & Cat Trust** website that deal with car seat safety for young children. The parent pages are free to access, but in the secure area there are some good lesson plans for teachers and other professionals on keeping safe.

Once he is old enough to understand, allow him to explore the car with you. He should only ever be allowed to move round the car with an adult, and the engine should always be off. Try to convey the impression that the inside of the car is soft and comfortable. Show him where the driver sits, the position of the steering wheel and where he sits in relation to the driver. Then show him the outside of the car, and the cold, hard metal that would hurt him if it hit him. Compare his size with the size of the car and reinforce safety procedures.

8.01–8.02: PAVEMENTS ARE FOR PEOPLE, ROADS ARE FOR VEHICLES

As you go out and about on foot, reinforce to your child that pavements are for people, and roads are for vehicles. If a vehicle is on the pavement, explain to him that it shouldn't be! Also, that pedestrians should only cross roads after careful consideration. He can start learning the basics of road safety even while still in his buggy, but he needs his parents and carers to set a good example. Talk to him about where you are going, and describe and name anything he might encounter – this compensates for the loss of incidental learning. Say things like, 'Down the kerb, onto the road' or 'Up the kerb, onto the pavement'. These terms will gradually be put into context.

Once he is walking, use reins or a wrist link to keep him close to you and safe. He shouldn't be allowed to free-walk until you are certain you have established voice control and are positive that he will respond immediately to 'Stop'. A small child should still hold your hand whenever you are near a road. Unless there is a particular reason, keep your child on the side furthest away from the road. Continue to talk to him as you travel, and give him the vocabulary he will need to learn about road safety. You can use the 'Mobility adventure walk' (Busy Bag 7, pages 108–109) and progress onto the 'Urban trail' (Activity Sheet 16, pages 167–171), to make sure you cover as many elements as possible. There is also 'Stop, look and listen', a road safety handout for parents, with basic prompts (Handout 14, page 202). Make yourself familiar with the Green Cross Code and use it, as your child will model his behaviour on yours.

8.03: MAIN VEHICLES

If you have a car, your child will already be familiar with cars and the noises they make. Listen to the traffic yourself and see what differences in sound you can hear and which vehicles you can successfully identify. Pick out a handful to start with and concentrate on them.

Lorries are noisy, have a low rumble, rattle, and sound heavy on the road. Modern cars have a more medium pitch and rarely rattle. Motorbikes, depending on the engine size, either have a higher-pitched 'Phut' or a throaty roar. Decide together what they sound like. Begin with these, although you can also include buses, particularly if you use them.

Along with these vehicles, talk about emergency vehicles, which young children seem to find particularly appealing. These are no longer so easy to identify from their sirens, but there are other clues you can use. Currently, only fire engines use air horns, so if they use them (together with the fact that they sound more like lorries) this makes them more easily identifiable. The police mainly use cars, so if there is a siren and it sounds like a car, it is probably the police. That leaves the ambulance as the other emergency vehicle sound. There are exceptions – paramedics and fire personnel do travel in cars – but these are unusual, so don't overload your child with rarities.

Check online to see if your local fire station runs open days. These are used as fundraisers and for awareness raising. They often offer children the opportunity to climb in the cab and to try equipment, both of which bring home to your child the size of the truck and enhances his knowledge. As a bonus, you often find other emergency teams may be present.

When you finally get to road crossings, point out to your child that emergency vehicles may be moving faster than other vehicles and may not be able to stop. Therefore, they should never cross if an emergency siren is sounding. A number of sounds games are commercially available. Twinkl produces several transport activities and bingo games you can use with your child as you introduce traffic sounds.

If your child has some useful vision, he may well be able to identify buses and lorries by size or the blocks of colour. Some children see or respond to certain colours better than others, so make use of that if you can. There is a difference between the sounds of buses or lorries. Help your child to differentiate between them by standing near a bus stop and letting him hear the swish of the bus doors as passengers alight.

Making your child aware of different traffic, as part of early road safety awareness, helps him develop listening skills. As a child with a sight impairment, he is going to be more dependent on listening skills to cross the road safely. As a progression, get him to indicate where the sound is coming from or which way it is going. Can he tell you when the vehicle is right next to him? This is enhancing his awareness that the vehicle is moving, and introducing the notion of speed and distance. A sighted child cannot securely judge speed and distance of vehicles until around age 10, whereas a child with a sight impairment will need a great deal of practice to judge speed and distance effectively.

Table 8.2 First vehicles

Car	Lorry	Motorbike
Police car	Fire	Ambulance
	Bus	

Table 8.3 Expansion vehicles

Tractor	Bin lorry	Scooter
Train	Boat	Cycle
Aeroplane	Helicopter	Tram

8.04–8.05: SAFER PLACES TO CROSS, PUSH BUTTON ON PELICAN

There are many ways to get from one side of the road to the other. Some don't require you to step into the road at all, so try and help your child experience them all. Subways and underpasses have fallen out of favour, but can still be found in large cities. Footbridges provide another way of reaching the other side without touching the road. Make a point of investigating whether the traffic sounds are above or below you. However you are crossing, you should make sure that he holds your hand and you both apply 'Stop, look and listen' at every crossing.

Remember: At this age your child should just be experiencing good road safety practice, not applying the strategies and techniques himself. Even if a child only has a small amount of useful vision, encourage him to use it, as it will support the decision-making process.

Table 8.4 Safer ways to cross

STOP, LOOK AND LISTEN	ZEBRA	PELICAN
Hold hands	Crossing patrol (lollipop)	Puffin
Footbridge	Subway	Toucan
Traffic island	Police	Pegasus

How many of these safer ways to cross do you know about and fully understand? All this information can be found in the Highway Code (you can buy a printed version quite inexpensively, or download it from www.highwaycodeuk.co.uk/download-pdf.html).

Most children get confused between zebra and pelican crossings, but it important to know the different ways they work. Young children should concentrate early road safety on controlled crossings that make the vehicle stop to allow pedestrians to cross.

Pelican Crossing

Pelicans are the most common type of controlled crossing. Draw your child's attention to the blister (tactile) paving on the ground that indicates a crossing point. However, do be aware that that it can also be installed at other crossing points that are inappropriate for someone with a vision impairment.

The pedestrian pushes the button on the pole, which in turn lights the 'Wait' sign. If your child can't see the red and green person on the opposite pavement, he may be able to see the illuminated

'Wait' sign, which will go out when it is time to cross. After the traffic lights turn to red, the traffic should stop. The green person on the other side of the road will then light up, and the beeps will sound to indicate that it is safe to cross. Make sure your child understands that traffic lights are for vehicles and the red and green people are for pedestrians. If he can see colours, spend some time working on red and green, so that he recognises them reliably.

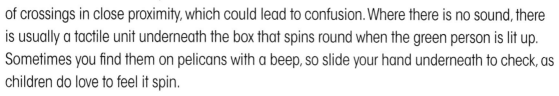

Occasionally, a pelican will not emit beeps when it is safe to cross. This is usually because there are a number of crossings in close proximity, which could lead to confusion. Where there is no sound, there is usually a tactile unit underneath the box that spins round when the green person is lit up. Sometimes you find them on pelicans with a beep, so slide your hand underneath to check, as children do love to feel it spin.

A number of pelicans have been replaced by puffin crossings. Puffins work on the same basic principles, but the indicator to cross is on the post, rather than the red and green person on the opposite side of the road. This means that you have to stand adjacent to the post in order to see when it changes. There are two types of shared use crossings: toucans allow pedestrians and cyclists to cross together, and pegasus (or equestrian) crossings are designed for horse riders and pedestrians.

Toucan crossing

Zebra crossings require a more complex decision-making process, so are more difficult for children. The pedestrian should stop at the kerb and wait for the traffic to stop. This can be difficult because sometimes the traffic on one side stops, but continues to run on the other side. Using hearing alone, it can be very difficult, and take a considerable amount of time, to make a decision to cross on a zebra. Unfortunately, the perception of time for drivers is rather different from that of pedestrians, and sometimes the driver loses patience with the decision-making process just at the point where the child decides it might be safe to cross. For this reason, children should repeatedly rehearse zebra crossing decision making with adult support, to help them refine and speed up the decision-making process. Encourage him to wave thanks to the driver, as this often mitigates for the perceived delay in crossing.

Every time you use a pelican crossing (or other controlled crossing), get your child to press the button and then tell you when it's safe to cross. If you use a zebra, make sure he stands where he can be clearly seen by oncoming traffic. Rehearse the decision-making process together and get him to use and refine his listening skills to ascertain whether vehicles are moving or stationary.

8.06: EARLY ENVIRONMENTAL AWARENESS, TEXTURES AND GRADIENTS

While you and your child are out and about, continue to build your child's awareness of the environment around him. Point out changes in depth, surface and gradient, for these are how he will navigate and orientate himself in the future. Try Activity 14, 'Post a letter' (pages 162–163), to give yourselves a reason to go out and explore the local area. If you usually drive, take him on a bus, just for the fun of it. Get him to walk from the front to the back, to give him an idea how long a bus is in comparison with a car, and explore the upstairs, too. In some locations, you may find warning strips at the top of steps and stairs, and also that the bus stop is indicated by some sort of tactile paving.

If your child trips up kerbs, try to remember to give him advance warning, and make sure you say whether it's up or down. If your child has useful vision, get him to look out for any double yellow lines, as they will also indicate approximately where the kerb is. If your child is already a cane user, he should use it (rather than his feet) to detect all these changes at ground level.

If you are uncertain about any of the road safety strategies mentioned here, speak to your habilitation specialist.

9.00: Personal safety

9.00	SIMPLE PERSONAL SAFETY STRATEGIES
9.01	Protective behaviours
9.02	NSPCC PANTS rule
9.03	My name, your name
9.04	Safer strangers (people who help us)
9.05	Uniforms
9.06	Understand, respond to and use 'No'
9.07	Understand and respond to 'Stop'
9.08	Lost child

Activities to work on these skills

See 'Useful websites' below for a range of activities to work on these skills.

Activity Sheet: 14 Post a letter

Handout

15 I'm lost!

Useful websites

➢ NSPCC PANTS rule: www.nspcc.org.uk/preventing-abuse/keeping-children-safe/underwear-rule/

➢ Protective Behaviours: www.safety-net.org.uk/protective-behaviours/

➢ Safety information for 4–7s: www.thinkuknow.co.uk/4_7/

➢ Child Safe Zones: www.100ways.org.uk/child-safe-zones-and-lost-children.html

➢ Clever Never Goes: www.safe4me.co.uk/portfolio/clever-never-goes/

➢ In an emergency: www.wmfs.net/safety/emergency/

➢ Dog, Duck & Cat: www.dogduckandcat.co.uk/

> Child Accident Prevention Trust: www.capt.org.uk/

> Twinkl activity sheets https://www.twinkl.co.uk/

Useful books and videos

Jean and Gareth Adamson (2011), *Topsy and Tim, Safety First* (Ladybird Books).

Steve Cox (2012), *Is That You, Wolf?* (BES Publishing).

Goldilocks and the Three Bears

Little Red Riding Hood

Historically, we have always taught children about 'stranger danger', but this is a confusing term and has fallen out of favour recently. Current thinking leans towards 'safer strangers' or developing the theme of 'people who help us'. Children need to recognise that Strangers are not all bad – indeed, you need to trust some strangers – but by the same token, some people you know may not have your best interests at heart. In order to understand and recognise risky situations, your child needs to understand emotions. The challenge is to build understanding and develop personal safety strategies without creating unnecessary anxiety, for both children and parents. Your child is unlikely to go anywhere alone until he is older, so this is preparatory work. This chapter ties in with the new statutory RSE (Relationships and Sex Education) curriculum.

If your child has a vision impairment, reinforce any strategies that he needs to keep himself safe. This might include using his cane (if he has one) or wearing his spectacles so he can better see hazards around him. Teach him about the dangers of traffic (see 8.00, 'Road safety', pages 74–80) and the risks associated with water.

9.01: PROTECTIVE BEHAVIOURS

These days, many children are taught about Protective Behaviours in school. They learn that they have the right to feel safe and that nothing is too awful or too small to talk to someone about. The Protective Behaviours programme offers a strategy for life (not a quick fix), but helps the child recognise emotions that emerge when they feel unsafe and then provides a strategy to resolve the situation. You can find more about this comprehensive programme on the Protective Behaviours website (www.safety-net.org.uk/protective-behaviours/), or from your child's school (if your child is learning about it).

Your child needs to recognise the emotions she experiences when she feels safe, and those she feels when not safe. It may be helpful to address this before your child starts school, as it may take her some time to absorb. The range of emotions can be difficult for a child with SVI to grasp (without the reinforcement of facial expressions and body language), so you may need to rely on intonation and description to convey emotion. Ask her where and when she feels safe. This is a difficult concept and may need some time to extract. If you can establish with her what feeling safe is like, you can move on to 'It's fun to feel scared'. Again, this might need some teasing out, but you can use hide-and-seek, or playing boo or tig (tag). If she really doesn't like it, she can say no, so help her learn that she is in control. Taking control makes the scared feeling go away. This scared feeling is one of the body's early warning signs. If your child can recognise these early warning signs, or gut instincts, she will know when she should do something, or when she needs to seek help, to make herself feel safe again.

Children are encouraged to talk to their network, the set of predetermined adults who will listen and support them with every concern, no matter how big or small. Ask your child who she would talk to if she didn't feel safe at school or nursery. We all relate better to some people than others. Having established this dialogue, it makes it easier to address some of the more difficult strategies that are necessary to keep your child safe.

If your child struggles with these complex emotions, it may be helpful to spend some time on the more obvious emotions and developing some emotion language. Lots of children in the autistic spectrum struggle with emotions and expressing them, and many children with SVI also show autistic traits and take things quite literally until they learn more about the world. Talk to your child about what makes her feel happy and sad or angry. When she recounts events, give her the emotional language that fits the scenario – for instance, 'I bet that made you feel cross' or 'That must have been frustrating for you'. Then share what makes you feel that way. It is helpful to share emotions using clear language. Don't say 'You make me angry', say 'I feel angry when you do that'. **Emotional literacy** is the term used to describe the ability to understand and express feelings. It requires children to recognise their own feelings and manage them, and is a skill they all need to develop.

9.02: THE NSPCC PANTS RULE

The NSPCC PANTS website (www.nspcc.org.uk/preventing-abuse/keeping-children-safe/underwear-rule/) sends a very similar message to the Protective Behaviours programme, but in a more light-hearted framework.

PANTS STANDS FOR:

Privates are private
Always remember your body belongs to you
No means no
Talk about secrets that upset you
Speak up, someone can help

The website has resources for parents and schools, as well as the Pantosaurus song to reinforce learning. The NSPCC have also created a new Amazon Alexa app for PANTS that makes it even more accessible to children with vision impairments. Open your Alexa app and enable the NSPCC skill. Ask Alexa to 'Open NSPCC', then ask her to 'Play the PANTS song' or 'Start the PANTS game'.

The PANTS rule talks about 'Privates', which is clear. Remember, however, that correct anatomical terms are recommended, even from Year 1.

9.03: MY NAME, YOUR NAME

If you and your child are out and about – and hopefully you will be – you can become separated in the most unexpected places. Children can fit under fixtures and fittings and, if they don't respond when called, they can appear to be missing for some time.

Make sure your child knows his own name and the real names (not just 'Mummy' or 'Auntie') of at least one primary carer. If your child is able to learn his address, or even just part of it, that is also helpful in getting him restored to you quickly. Some parents put their child's name into outerwear and inside bags. However, it's not a good idea to buy your child goods or clothing that display their name, because children with SVI or a learning difficulty may assume that they already know someone who comes up to them and uses their name.

Rehearse names and addresses using Activity Sheet 14 ('Post a letter', pages 162–163). This helps to reinforce understanding of a home address, as well as introduces the child to the postal system.

9.04–9.05: SAFER STRANGERS, PEOPLE WHO HELP US (UNIFORMS)

While parents want to keep their children safe, it is important to recognise that children are rarely abducted and even more rarely are they taken by strangers. In fact, people they know pose a greater risk to them. For this reason, children need to be made aware of risks and given strategies to use which neither make them unnecessarily fearful nor restrict healthy interaction with the world around them. The strategies listed above cover some ways of equipping him to deal with difficult situations, but you may need to cover a wider variety of situations.

The term 'safer strangers' is used in preference to 'stranger danger' to reflect the fact that some strangers have to be trusted. These safer strangers usually wear uniforms and offer some sort of help. They include police, ambulance and fire personnel, doctors and nurses, dentists and (less obviously) shop workers – people who help us. Twinkl produces some really good activities to develop this topic.

Clever Never Goes is another strategy. Introduced in 2018 in Hampshire, with the support of the Hampshire Constabulary, it moves the focus away from strangers and teaches children that they do not go with anyone unless it is prearranged. It builds children's abilities to deal with the wider world and boosts parents' confidence to let them have more independence.

Don't teach your child to fear strangers – most would only want to help. Instead, work together to create a list of safe people that he would be allowed to go with. Clever Never Goes means you never go anywhere with anyone not on that list, unless it has been planned by a parent or carer.

In the event of a problem, teach your child to approach the safest stranger he can find. This could be a police officer, a shop assistant or a parent with a pram. This does not mean go anywhere with them. Teach your child:

> Shout 'No!' Then run away, yell 'Help' and tell a grown-up.

9.06–9.07: UNDERSTAND, RESPOND TO AND USE 'NO' AND 'STOP'

In any emergency situation, it is important that your child understands 'No' and 'Stop' and will respond to them. It can be equally important for him to be able to use them. As a general rule, children are expected to be polite and well behaved, but rules are there to protect us and can be broken in a real emergency. Use the phrase **'No, Run, Yell, Tell'** to reinforce this.

9.08: LOST CHILD

if you and your child become separated, have you got an pre-agreed procedure that you both will follow? It can save a great deal of stress and anxiety if you have planned for this before it actually happens. Your child can wander off in just a moment – maybe while you are loading the trolley or dealing with a sibling. Most children are not lost, but are simply obscured from view, particularly if they are small and in a crowded shop. A child with a vision impairment is more likely to lose sight of a parent or carer, so it is even more important to establish procedures and rehearse them. Encourage him to stay close and, if he does become separated, to stay still.

Use Handout 15 ('I'm Lost!', page 203) as a starting point and adapt it to suit your family and your locality. Some shopping centres run Safe Child schemes, so it may suit you to tap into those procedures.

While you are in a big shop, talk to your child about what he can do if you become separated and point the tills out to him. Practise locating the tills from different points in a shop, so he knows where to go. Remind him that he must never leave the store, except with his named safe people or a police officer.

If you are really anxious about becoming separated from your child, consider disposable safety ID wristbands, or personalised silicone wristbands. When he is older, you may like to consider a smart GPS tracker before allowing him to have a mobile phone. Children don't need mobile phones before they start travelling independently, and just carrying one can make them vulnerable. If you do give your child a phone, go for an older model that has little or no street value.

Other ways to keep your child safe

➢ Emergency services – does your child know how to call the emergency services and what each branch does? Rehearse procedures for calling them. 999 is the traditional number in this country, but 112 also works in the UK and throughout Europe (and a child with a vision impairment finds it easier to locate 1 and 2). Teach your child to use a landline if you still have one – these are easier to key in and make it simpler for the emergency services to locate you. Make sure he realises the number is for genuine emergencies only. Search online for practice calls, as well.

➢ Make sure your child knows what the smoke alarm sounds like and what to do if it goes off. Plan your escape routes and rehearse them. Instil in him:

   Get out, stay out, call the Fire Service out!

➢ Teach your child to have a healthy fear of things that will injure (see also 8.00, 'Road safety', pages 74–80). Fire and water – both at home and outside – are the most obvious risks, but there are many things in the home that are dangerous. Investigate the Child Accident Prevention Trust (CAPT) website for more information on risks and how to reduce them. The **Dog Duck & Cat Trust** provides information, activities and stories to help discuss these risks with your child.

➢ Tiny cell batteries, often found in toys or electronic devices, are extremely dangerous. These tend to be in things that young children gravitate towards, like remote controls, car keys, light and sound toys. It is a particular problem if you have a child who likes to explore by putting objects in his mouth, and children aged between 1 and 4 are most at risk. These batteries can block the food pipe and cause catastrophic burns.

➢ Detergent capsules, used in washing machines and dishwashers, come in bright attractive designs and are not sold in childproof containers. While generally they may be kept behind a child-locked cupboard door, it takes no time at all for your child to help himself from the box as you are loading the washer. As well as being highly poisonous, the capsule can burst when bitten, and squirt detergent into the eyes (causing permanent damage).

➢ Try to keep your floor free of clutter, to reduce the risk of your child tripping. You can buy cushioned corners for tables or other obstacles. Some are clear (to be aesthetically pleasing), but others are in stronger colours that will make the corner more visible to the child. If the table merges with the colour of the floor, add a contrasting runner or a piece of Dycem® mat to increase visibility.

10.00: Starting school or nursery

10.00	STARTING SCHOOL OR NURSERY
10.01	Willingness to separate from primary carer
10.02	Early orientation mobility skills
10.03	Developing dressing skills
10.04	Locate and use coat peg
10.05	Locate and use toilets
10.06	Locate dining area
10.07	Cope with school meal or lunch box
10.08	Access playground
10.09	Social interaction with peers
10.10	Asking for help

Activities to work on these skills

Busy Bag: 1 LLI (liquid level indicator) – pouring

Activity Sheets: 1 I can fasten 1, 2 I can fasten 2, 15 All about me

Prerequisite skills

If your child struggles with any of these activities, refer back to earlier chapters.

Handouts

4 Dressing tricks and tips, 6 Supporting cold pouring

Online resources: 5 Essential social skills checklist 8 Ready for school assessment checklist

Useful websites

➢ Is my child ready for school: www.bbc.co.uk/bitesize/articles/zv76jhv

➢ BBC starting primary school: www.bbc.co.uk/bitesize/collections/starting-primary-school/1

➢ Starting primary school with SEND BBC Bitesize: www.bbc.co.uk/bitesize/articles/zv8q8xs

Useful books

Jean Adamson and Gareth Adamson (2009), *Topsy and Tim Start School* (Ladybird Books).

Lauren Child (2015), *I Am Too Absolutely Small for School* (Orchard Books).

Hélène Hilton (ed.) (2018), *Stuff to Know When You Start School* (Dorling Kindersley).

Some children are clearly ready for school and can't wait to go, while others find the whole idea overwhelming. However, each child is different, regardless of any disability. It can also be traumatic for some parents, who are anxious about handing their child over to the care of someone else. If you are worried, try not to let your child pick up on it. Present information in such a way that helps her look forward to the start of school. Most schools will gradually phase children in, splitting the class into morning or afternoon attendance. They will have some sessions in the summer term for new September starters, too. If necessary, your **habilitation specialist** may be able to arrange additional visits.

School may well provide an introductory pack for your child. If not, make sure you go through the 'Ready for school assessment checklist' (Online Resource 8) and prepare her as well as you can. As she probably can't read yet, ask if your child's school can provide you with a photograph of her teacher and any teaching assistants – schools usually know which class children are going into before breaking up for the summer.

To make a successful transition into school, your child will need to bring together all the skills from the previous nine chapters. They are all closely intertwined, so there is crossover and repetition, and some skills may need to be revisited (depending on your child's developmental maturity). You may find your child can demonstrate these skills in certain settings but cannot transfer them into new ones. This may mean you have to cover the same ground, but with a different focus, in order to make it more school-specific.

Mainstream schools and nurseries can expect support from local authority specialists (like a **QTVI** or habilitation specialist) to ensure the child can access the curriculum and move around safely. They can provide direct training to staff, as well as the child's peer group. The QTVI will advise on adapting materials, producing large print or Braille or Moon for the child, as well as recommending the best place for the child to sit in class. The habilitation specialist will advise on mobility, orientation and independent living skills programmes. One of these professionals should undertake an environmental audit of the school before your child starts. If your child is going into a **resource base** or **special school,** there will be specialist staff on site. Visit different schools before selecting the one that best meets your child's needs, but remember that your child will need an **EHCP** (Education Health and Care Plan) to secure a place in a special school.

10.01: SEPARATION FROM PRIMARY CARER

Separation can be difficult for any child. Try to make sure your child goes to the local baby and toddlers group, so she gets used to wandering off without you. If your child is SVI, chances are she will be used to being close to you all the time, so find ways of separating beforehand. These include:

➢ Making a point of going into different rooms.

➢ Getting a friend or relative to babysit.

➢ Seeing if school has a playgroup or day care facility that can offer short-term care. (If not, you may have to negotiate with school to gradually build up her time in school.)

➢ Dropping her round to a friend or relative.

Practise making goodbye short and sweet, but always reassure her you will be back soon. Don't linger. If she is upset, school will deal with the situation best if you are not there.

10.02: EARLY ORIENTATION AND MOBILITY AROUND SCHOOL

As the transition point from home to school is so major, you should receive support from a habilitation specialist. He can visit school before your child starts, make her familiar with the classroom layout and help her to find her peg, the toilets and the dining room. This will also provide an opportunity for her to meet staff and for staff to be offered training to ease her transition into school. Foundation stage often has separate, discreet access to the school, which reduces the number of children milling around and provides simplified access to the teaching area.

10.03: DEVELOPING DRESSING SKILLS

It will be really beneficial to your child if you have already introduced independent dressing skills. Many children start school or nursery unable to undertake simple dressing tasks, but staff are often stretched getting everyone ready to go outside to play. It will be easier and calmer if your child can undertake at least some dressing skills independently.

Practise putting her coat on and taking it off (see 2.00, 'Dressing, undressing and fastenings', pages 17–26), and hanging her coat up. Make sure her coat has a good, sturdy loop to hang it from, and find a way to put her name inside in a way that she can recognise. You can sew something into the back like a shaped button or maybe add some French knots onto the label. Consider doing something similar for her PE kit. It is easier to put a coat on if it fits loosely, so maybe buy a size above if your child needs lots of layers. Also, if you are choosing a coat with a zip, try the zip before you buy, just to make sure it glides easily. Remember: Double-ended zips or coats with two zipped layers (such as a fleece inside the coat) may make it extremely difficult for your child to distinguish one piece of clothing from another.

If her uniform has a sweatshirt, make sure she is well practised putting it on and taking it off before she starts school. Children lose clothes at school all the time, but if something is hard to put on it frequently just gets left somewhere, never to be seen again! If she struggles with a particular set of buttons, try swapping them for smaller ones that go through the buttonhole more easily.

Shoes and wellies often find their way onto the wrong feet. It's not a big deal in the short term: if her feet are hurting, she'll probably realise. Praise her for putting her own footwear on and change them round when a suitable opportunity arises. When you swap them over, remind her of the way the shoes are shaped to match her feet and show her where the fastenings sit for those shoes. If the habit persists, try putting a durable shoe name label consistently in one foot and get her into the routine of always putting that shoe on first. Alternatively, mark the inside border of each shoe or boot with a subtle tactile marker (something like the RNIB's Tacti-Mark), or maybe stick something soft inside. Your child can then place the two marks together, to make sure they are the correct way round.

10.04: LOCATE AND USE COAT PEG

Because most children cannot read when they start school, it is common to use symbols or pictures to indicate coat pegs. Ask for a tactile symbol or a distinctive texture for your child. This doesn't need to be expensive or complicated – it could be sandpaper, a Velcro® strip or a piece of fluffy material. Suggest that she is allocated an end peg, as this avoids her having to search through a line of coats. Something equivalent could be done to identify the correct classroom door, particularly if your child uses a tactile timetable or objects of reference.

10.05: LOCATE AND USE TOILETS

Foundation stage usually have toilets close to, or immediately off, the teaching area. The habilitation specialist will make your child familiar with the route to the toilets, and their layout. However, it is really helpful if your child already knows how to use a toilet and wash her hands. Look at '3.00: Personal hygiene' (pages 27–35) for ideas to support your child with this. Ideally, school will have doors that contrast with the cubicle frame and a contrasting splashback behind the washbasin. These will help your child to use her vision to move around the bathroom. Request that the signage is placed at child's eye level and is tactile in some way, so she is sure she is entering the correct bathroom. Sometimes, children are too busy to go to the toilet or can't find them quickly enough, and accidents can (and do) happen. Put a plastic bag with spare underwear in her bag, just in case.

10.06: LOCATE DINING AREA

The route to and from the dining area will probably be taught by your habilitation specialist, but not necessarily before your child starts school. It really depends how much information your child has already had to absorb and how well it has been retained. It could be your child is guided to and from the dining hall and supported throughout the process of choosing dinner and taking the tray to the table, for example. If your child goes to the same seat every day, preferably on the end of a row, this makes access easier – speak to the person who is supporting your child through this process. It would be helpful to change the tray or plate colours, to provide maximum contrast with the food. For some children, particularly those with sensory issues, the dining hall is just too noisy an environment. In this case, it can be useful to go in first – so it is quieter and the noise levels gradually rise – rather than entering a dining hall that's at full volume.

Practise using a tray at home. Load it with something that will move if tipped, but not too heavy or too easily tipped, so the child can understand the need to keep a tray level. To start with a number of pompoms or scrunched paper balls work well. After a while, add something a bit heavier or more likely to tip. Try ping-pong balls or toy cars to get that extra movement, then add extra height and weight with rolling items on plastic plates and beakers. Paper cups, when not weighted with liquid, also tip easily.

10.07: COPE WITH SCHOOL MEAL OR LUNCH BOX

Your child will be supported into the dining room and when obtaining her lunch, but in order to eat confidently and well she will need at least basic cutlery skills. Refer back to '4.00: Feeding' (pages 36–44) if she still struggles with cutlery. School cutlery makes no concessions for small hands, so liaise with school and see what they are using in the dining hall if she struggles in school but not at home. Dinner supervisors may be able to cut up her food. However, they will need to know how to help her find the food on her plate, so share your home systems with school. If the problem persists, investigate smaller shaped cutlery or ask for an OT (occupational therapist) assessment.

If your child has a lunch box, make sure she can open it competently before going to school. Think about the contents of the lunch box and don't introduce new foods or packaging before trying at home. Many young children need help opening packaging, but if you practise beforehand, your child will be much more independent.

Use a drinks flask or a sports bottle in preference to cartons or pouches (which require her to insert a straw). This is difficult for any small child, but really challenging without useful vision. Inserting straws in pouches requires a particular knack that eludes most small children (and some adults!).

Practise pouring at home, so she can get her own drink. When practising, use a small vessel to start with and build up gradually (school water jugs are heavy for little hands). Sports bottle lids restrict the flow and make it easier for a child to be in control, and smaller bottles are lighter and easier to grasp. If your child has useful vision, try putting a ping-pong ball in a cup and watch it float up as the water goes in to develop an understanding of empty and full.

Crisp packets require a well-developed pincer grip and a degree of force to pull the sides apart. If she struggles with this – if it goes wrong, the contents can easily spread across the room – open the packet yourself when preparing the lunch box, and clip it closed with a peg or food clip. Choose fillings that will stay in the sandwich – for example, use sliced rather than grated cheese.

10.08: ACCESS PLAYGROUND

Playground access can present problems for a number of reasons. Schools may be anxious and feel that your child is vulnerable outside with hundreds of other children running around. Get your habilitation specialist or QTVI on board to present alternative strategies to the school. Bringing your child inside or providing one-to-one support isolates her and makes it more difficult for her to form friendships. All children need fresh air and the opportunity to run around. Your child should only stay inside if there are genuine medical reasons to do so.

Ask school to consider establishing a friendship stop, where children can meet one another in a less busy area of the playground. If ball games are allowed, suggest that they are confined to one area of the playground, and well away from the friendship stop. If the school wants an adult to support your child outside, suggest that he works as a play coordinator and draws other children into structured games.

Make sure your child has some understanding of basic playground games. Play games at home that require turn taking and sharing. Teach her how to count, so she can join in 'What's the time, Mr Wolf?' and hide-and-seek.

10.09: SOCIAL INTERACTION WITH PEERS

Try the 'Essential social skills' questionnaire (Online Resource 5) to give you an idea of what to work on. Your child will not be able to do everything on the list, but social skills are a work in progress as her knowledge and experience grows. She will need good social skills to make friends and deal with potential problems like bullying. Many social skills can be modelled through play. Refer back to 9.00, 'Personal safety' (pages 81–86) for information on developing **emotional literacy.**

Expect your child to display good manners and say 'Please' and 'Thank you', as well as to use appropriate greetings. A little politeness goes a long way and costs nothing. Help her to understand her own feelings, to better understand and empathise with other children. Encouraging her to be more empathetic will make her less likely to bully others, as she will recognise how others might feel.

Mainstream primary classes frequently gather on the carpet for circle time or stories. If you can, show her how to fold her arms and sit cross-legged on the floor. This is something that children usually learn by mimicking others. Start off sitting on the floor with her legs outstretched, then bend the knee, bring one foot into the centre and tuck it under her thigh. Then bend the other knee and tuck her other foot under the first bent knee. You may find she struggles to maintain this position, particularly if she has low muscle tone or poor core stability. Use the position at home for story time (or other activities) to get her used to it. If she still struggles, go back to activities that develop core stability, balance and strength, or seek specialist advice.

10.10: ASKING FOR HELP

Help her to become more assertive and teach her how to use a big voice rather than a whisper. This will help her to resist bullying and stand up for herself. If she is too loud, try to help her modulate the volume, so she doesn't intimidate others. Friendships are very important. They build self-esteem, make children feel more secure, help them achieve more and make them happier.

Activities you can try

➢ Name feelings for your child. Get her to talk about feelings as they arise, and name them. If she will sit through a film, try *Inside Out* (2015, Pixar) and chat about the emotions and what they are called.

➢ Use facial expressions when playing – if your child is SVI, you may have to describe them or let her feel your face.

➢ Use intonation or tone of voice to emphasise different emotions. This works particularly well when storytelling.

➢ Practise manners together and model the behaviour you expect from your child. Use imaginative role play. Act out some simple scenarios (such as asking for a toy), to show the different feelings provoked (and the results achieved) by being polite or being rude.

➢ Praise all empathetic behaviour.

If she has learned to recognise and speak about her emotions, your child is more likely to be able to seek help appropriately.

Part three

Appendices

Appendix 1: Busy Bags

These Busy Bags can be used for activity ideas or can be printed out and sent home for repetition. Each Busy Bag outlines the resources you need. All equipment is inexpensive and easily obtainable. If you are going to use a Busy Bag repeatedly, laminate the sheet and keep it in a zipped folder, together with the resources used.

Busy Bag 1
LLI (liquid level indicator) – pouring

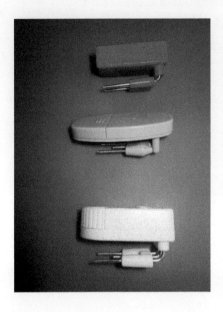 

RESOURCES

Liquid level indicator (LLI), tray, mug, jug for liquid

DIRECTIONS

Teach your child about pouring liquids. Simply place the LLI on the side of a mug. The sensors will let you know when the liquid gets to the top, through a series of beeping sounds and vibrations.

Add water to the first, intermittent beep and stop pouring. Add your squash to the second, faster, continuing beep. Stir and drink!

THINGS TO CONSIDER

Note: Only use cold drinks or water for this task. Hot drinks need to be introduced to a child *only* when age and ability appropriate. Always use mugs: they are more sturdy, and also have the benefit of a handle.

If your child has residual vision, think about contrast. Pour dark liquids (e.g. blackcurrant squash) into white mugs and lighter liquids (e.g. milk) into darker mugs. Encourage your child always to use a tray when pouring. This will help contain any spillages and make it easier to clean up!

It may help to decant squash into a smaller, more manageable pouring container like a sports bottle. This reduces the speed of the flow and causes less spillage if knocked over.

ALTERNATIVES

If you do not feel your child is ready for water, or you just fancy a change, try pouring lentils from a jug into a mug. Although this will not work with the LLI, lentils flow in a similar way, make a lovely noise and are more visible. Sand also pours well from one vessel to another, and can be mixed with water to create different consistencies and resistance.

Busy Bag 2
Edible sensory rattle

RESOURCES

Clean empty plastic bottle with lid (this can be any size, but preferably not too big, and a wider neck is easier), biscuits (if preferred, cereal or pieces of fruit), large rug or mat.

Note: Check first if the child has allergies or food intolerances, and take this into consideration when selecting the bottle's contents.

DIRECTIONS

Encourage your child to be involved in breaking up the biscuits and unscrewing the bottle lid. Sit on a large blanket – this allows for crumbs to be collected easily. Attempt to fit biscuits into the top of the bottle. Observe how your child manages with pieces that don't easily fit: they may happily move onto the next piece, or be determined to make each one fit. Then help your child to place the lid back on, and then explore – shake, roll, open, eat!

THINGS TO CONSIDER

This sensory activity is primarily about sound and listening, but also works on developing important fine motor skills. Use food your child likes, so that you build in an immediate reward.

Busy Bag 3
Peg and pompom painting

RESOURCES

Coloured pegs, small paint pots or yoghurt cartons, non-toxic paint, coloured pompoms, apron, messy play mat or tablecloth.

DIRECTIONS

Show your child how to 'pinch' the pompoms with a peg and then dip them into the paint. Stamp the paper with the pompoms and create patterns and shapes.

THINGS TO CONSIDER

Pinching objects like pompoms trains young children's finger muscles in preparation for higher-level fine motor tasks such as colouring with a crayon, cutting with scissors or writing with a pencil. This fine motor activity is an easy, gentle way to introduce little ones to finger painting, especially if they are nervous or extremely sensitive (sensory averse or tactile defensive) about getting messy. It provides a natural barrier between them and the paint, while still allowing them to participate actively in the process. A pincer grasp enables young children to feed themselves, as they are able to pick up small bits of food and place food in their mouth with ease.

First, experiment with pegs yourself, as some require more force than others to open.

As an alternative activity, how about cutting up some vegetables together and making vegetable prints? If you use a safety knife like the Kiddi Kutter, your child can join in. This requires a different kind of hand strength.

Busy Bag 4
Sock skills

RESOURCES

Loom bands or large hair scrunchies.

DIRECTIONS

Encourage your child to use both hands to stretch a hair scrunchie or loom band bracelet over their toes or feet, and then pull it up as far as their ankle. They can reverse the process to take it off, or – if they prefer – move onto another scrunchie. This activity requires many of the same processes and skills as putting socks on, but it is simplified and there is less resistance. Just as they would with socks, the child learns to stretch the opening over the toes and then to roll it over the foot to the ankle.

This activity develops hand strength and dexterity, builds the notion of spreading and stretching the fingers, and improves body awareness, attention and dressing skills.

THINGS TO CONSIDER

If the band or scrunchie leaves a mark on the skin, it is too small/tight. Fabric scrunchies/loom bands are better. If your child has useful vision, use well-saturated colours.

Using multicoloured scrunchies/loom bands makes this activity more fun, and offers the opportunity to learn about colours while the child practises. Fastening a small bell onto them can provide more entertainment, too.

Take a look at this video from Mama OT if you want to see how it's done: http://mamaot.com/clever-way-to-practice-putting-on-taking-off-socks

Busy Bag 5
Treasure baskets

 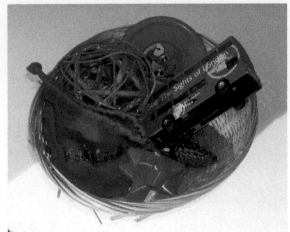

RESOURCES

A basket or box, and a variety of everyday things. Natural items work best (plastic feels like plastic, whatever its shape), but include items that you think will attract the child.

Examples: spoon, pastry brush, wooden eggcup, coaster, empty boxes (various sizes), wooden and metal curtain rings, glasses case, leather purse, avocado stone, bottle brush, velvet hairbands and scrunchies, orange, lemon, shells, cork, pine cone, shaving brush, tiny baskets, toothbrush, whistle, beads on a string, small bowls.

DIRECTIONS

Consider themes when making your treasure basket: colours, seasons, materials, textures, sounds, etc. The basket items should vary in weight, size, texture, colour, taste, temperature and sound, so that each item stimulates one or more of the five senses. Encourage your child to explore the treasure basket using their senses – discovering what an object is, what it is like, perhaps what it does when shaken or manipulated. Employ the 'WESST' strategy when exploring: weight, edges, size, shape (smell) and texture.

THINGS TO CONSIDER

Treasure baskets are particularly relevant for babies and young children who have a visual impairment (VI), because they can offer a range of direct hands-on sensory experiences. They offer a simple, fun and highly effective way to enrich the early experiences of children and parents can create them cheaply and easily at home. Change contents to avoid boredom – swap one or two things at a time initially, rather than changing wholescale, and gradually expand knowledge of items. Once the child is more confident, introduce completely new, themed baskets.

Busy Bag 6
Bath paint

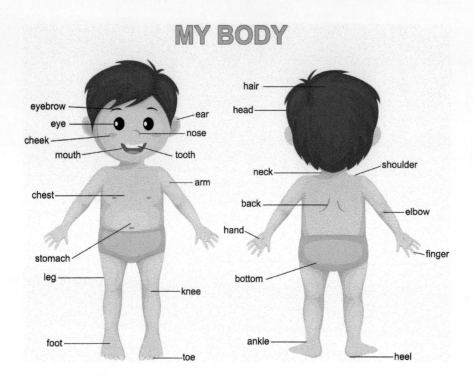

RESOURCES

Bath paints or bath crayons.

DIRECTIONS

Bath paints (or bath crayons) can be used in the bath to draw pictures or play number and letter games. Children can also try to guess the shape you draw on their back. Draw along the length of the arm/leg, adding each separate finger/toe, then give each body part its name. Discuss and name as many body parts as you can, and develop image concepts.

THINGS TO CONSIDER

Drawing with bath crayons is a fun idea. It is also great for working on fine motor skills, body awareness and body movement. Families can practise body awareness with little children naturally during bathtime and while getting dressed.

A mature and efficient grasp of the pencil will only develop if your child's other fine motor skills have developed properly. In particular, as you can see from following the link below, the thumb, index and middle fingers work together to control the pencil in what is called a dynamic tripod pencil grasp.

Moving through the different stages of pencil grasp development is an important part of early childhood development. This development usually moves through the palmar grip, then four- or five-finger pencil grip and finally the tripod pencil grip. Find out more here:

www.ot-mom-learning-activities.com/correct-pencil-grasp.html

Busy Bag 7
Mobility adventure walk

RESOURCES

Adventure walk information sheet.

DIRECTIONS

Go for a walk with your child and, while you are out and about, discuss your surroundings informally. Introduce words and concepts using ideas from 'Let's go on an adventure walk!' below. You can do this in any new environment, each time adding in new concepts.

Adventure walks are outdoor explorations and field trips turned into learning opportunities. Children who are severely vision impaired (SVI) or have low vision often miss important information about the world around them, especially in outdoor settings and public places. By helping them to get 'up close and personal' with objects, you can improve their understanding, increase their language opportunities and enrich their social exchanges with family and friends. A full memory bank of touching, hearing, smelling and looking at things outdoors and in the community will build important concepts for further learning. Children with SVI also increase their tactile tolerance and curiosity this way. Those with low vision enjoy the same benefits and expand their understanding of what they see.

THINGS TO CONSIDER

As well as missing important information about the world around them, children with SVI are at risk of colliding with obstacles, so it will help if they can become familiar with different obstacles and street furniture. The 'mobility' aspect of this activity refers to the ability to move safely, efficiently and effectively from one place to another – for instance, being able to walk simple routes without tripping or falling, eventually crossing roads safely and using public transport.

By introducing the 'wider environment' to your child as early as possible, you will be improving concept development, encouraging exploration of the environment and safety, as well as promoting independent travel. These explorations help make sense of the world and provide children with an introduction to landmarks and cues.

THINGS TO LOOK OUT FOR

Plants, flowers, trees, postbox, pavement, kerb, cars, grass, gravel, puddles, leaves, street signs, bins.

Listen to bird sounds, people chatting, traffic, tills in stores – the list is endless.

Progress onto Activity Sheet 16: Urban trail (page 167–171).

Let's go on an adventure walk!

Things your child can examine include: plants, flowers, trees, postbox, pavement, kerb, cars, grass, gravel and play equipment.

If he is small enough, pick up your child or get him close to each object, as this provides the option of touch. Tell him what the object is and touch it yourself. Tap the object to produce a sound, if possible. Discuss its material – is it wood, metal, plastic, etc.? Explain what the object is and how it is used, what it is for. This helps build environmental language.

Repeat these walks as often as you can. Vary the route, as this provides a variety of different objects to explore and discuss. Regular exposure should increase your child's interest and tolerance.

If your child walks, encourage him to move freely all over your garden or the playground. While you follow closely (in order to supervise), provide verbal interpretation of surfaces, sounds and objects. If it is safe to do so, let him contact obstacles with his hands or cane, instead of guiding him around them. Tell him what he is about to touch.

As your child explores, take note of what he especially enjoys and return to repeat these activities at a later date. He may prefer splashing in puddles, scraping his feet in the gravel or turning on the garden hose. Use whatever he loves most to make movement and exploring the outdoors meaningful and fun.

If your child does not yet move independently, provide a small familiar blanket from which she can explore grass, sand or bark. Let him explore the surfaces along the edge of the blanket in his own time.

Children often need extra motivation to play outdoors. At first, the outdoors may feel overwhelming. They will be dealing with unfamiliar sensations such as ground textures, air temperatures, breezes against the skin, and the sounds of animals, lawnmowers, traffic, amongst many others. Repeated experiences with enjoyable activities and play items may give your child a reason to explore the outdoors.

Children who are light sensitive or photophobic can enjoy playing outdoors with some simple precautions: make sure they wear a hat with a broad brim, use sunglasses and plenty of suncream, and encourage them to play in shaded areas.

Busy Bag 8
Spoon control

RESOURCES

Tray, two bowls or other similar vessels, porridge oats (or other dry cereal – using rice pops will also add a fun sound), a variety of spoons.

DIRECTIONS

This particular skill encourages accuracy to transfer and hand/eye coordination.

Encourage your child to feel the items in the tray and explore them. Discuss the different spooning utensils, such as their colour, size and texture. Feel the oats, and allow time to play before you demonstrate the skill of spooning the oats from one vessel to another. This may be by using the hand over hand method or verbal instructions. The tray will hopefully contain any spillage, but also allow an opportunity to gauge the success rate.

THINGS TO CONSIDER

Young children typically hold a spoon in a palmar or fist grip when they're first learning to feed themselves. That doesn't offer them a lot of control over the utensil – just enough to get whatever is in their bowl (usually a sticky sort of food) onto the spoon and into their mouth.

As their hands begin to develop more fine motor control, they will tend to hold the spoon more with their fingers than their fist. This helps them to manipulate the spoon in a more controlled way and therefore to transfer less sticky foods successfully.

Try not to send mixed messages to very small children. Therefore, if you are using a spoon, make sure that whatever they pick up is edible.

If the child cannot keep loose foodstuffs on the spoon, go back to stickier substances like Angel Delight or mashed potato. You can make your mash more colourful by adding carrot or replacing/mixing it with sweet potato.

Deeper spoons hold food better, whereas shallower spoons are easier to eat from.

Busy Bag 9
The money game

RESOURCES

A selection of coins appropriate to the child's age and ability, two dice, game sheet.

DIRECTIONS

Follow the instructions given on the next page. Handling money can be a challenge if you're severely vision impaired, as it's often difficult to tell the difference between coins. It is possible to identify coins by touch, although this may prove much more difficult for children with additional learning difficulties. Start with small denomination coins like the 1p and 2p. Do not add other coins until the child is secure with these. Repetition is vital.

THINGS TO CONSIDER

In the UK, it is possible to differentiate between coins using touch.

Familiarise yourself with each coin first, then introduce them to the child. Copper coins have smooth edges, and silver coins have ridges or a unique shape and size. For example, identify a 1p coin by its colour, size and smooth edge, and the sound it makes when dropped on the table. Identify a 10p by checking for the ridges on its side, its sound and size. Be consistent in the way you identify each coin. Allow the child to discover differences in each one. Independently identifying money can be challenging for children who are vision impaired. When teaching children to sort and identify coins, it is important to provide hands-on experience with real coins. Never use plastic coins, as they don't feel the same at all. As your child achieves greater knowledge of coins and value, increase the complexity of the game.

Add one new coin at a time, but only when the child can reliably identify the coins you have already introduced. You can modify the game by increasing the values of the rewards, or by getting the child to make suggestions for different scenarios.

The money game

INSTRUCTIONS

Choose the value of the coins you will play with and create scenarios to suit those coins. Use tactile dice if the child has a vision impairment.

Start with 1p and 2p coins first, and gradually introduce others as the child becomes more competent. This works really well in small groups, with an adult as the banker. The banker pays out and 'collects' on anything that doesn't directly relate to another player.

Give each player a pot or tray containing between 10 and 15 pence. The more money each player has, the longer the game can go on. The winner is the player with the most money. You can either count up the money after an agreed time, or when someone runs out of money. Players take it in turns to throw the dice. Look at the list of forfeits on the next page (some good, some bad!).

You can also play adult against child. The dice make it random, so the only skills are being able to count and to handle money.

The money game

Value of dice	Forfeit
2	You find 5p.
3	You have a hole in your pocket – lose 4p.
4	It's your birthday – get 2p.
5	You buy a magazine, which costs 5p.
6	The tooth fairy leaves you 3p.
7	Pocket money time! You get 6p.
8	Lend your friend 2p.
9	You buy some sweets, costing you 3p.
10	You drop some money – lose 5p.
11	A friend gives you 5p.
12	It's your lucky day! You win 2p.

Busy Bag 10
Use a whisk – make Angel Delight

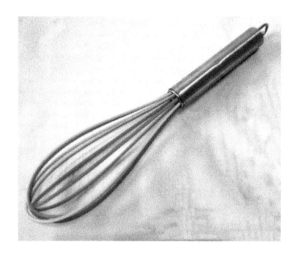

RESOURCES

Tray, whisk, mixing bowl, packet of Angel Delight (or equivalent), Dycem® non-slip mat.

DIRECTIONS

Teach your child about what a whisk is for and how it is used. Look at a variety of whisks (for example, electric, metal, nylon) so that they understand the concept, and demonstrate the 'whisking' action.

Master the whisking technique. Then hold the bowl at an angle, resting it on Dycem® mat, and make up the Angel Delight (using the packet instructions). Before it sets, maybe add fruit for extra texture and flavour, but do make sure the child gets to eat the fruits of their labour.

THINGS TO CONSIDER

Explore the qualities of different types of whisks. For example:

➢ Whisk bubbles in a bowl.

➢ Add a plastic whisk to the collection.

➢ Explore an electric hand whisk (NB Make sure it is not plugged in).

➢ Listen to the different sounds each whisk makes when used.

➢ Find out which is the heaviest, and lightest, whisk.

Dycem® mat is perfect for resting a bowl on, as it avoids slipping. It is also ideal for most crockery, especially when you are introducing eating skills to young children. It is also useful because it provides additional contrast between the bowl and surface.

Wherever possible, choose a brightly coloured whisk, and make sure you also choose a mixing bowl that contrasts with the colour of your mixture.

This activity ties in beautifully with Busy Bag 8: Spoon control (pages 111–112).

Useful link: www.dycem.com/

Busy Bag 11
Brushing teeth

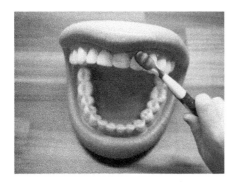

RESOURCES

Variety of toothbrushes (include manual, electric and battery brushes), variety of different toothpastes (flavours, colours), model of human teeth (if available), toothbrushing timers, 'This Is the Way We Brush Our Teeth' lyrics.

DIRECTIONS

Spend time familiarising the child with the objects above and the process of brushing teeth. See if you can find a brush that the child feels comfortable using. Give him time to explore his own teeth, using his finger. The little finger brushes are much easier for small hands.

Use the hand over hand method to encourage exploration of the mouth with the brush. If your child is now happy to try brushing, don't waste too much time or effort attempting to squeeze the paste onto the brush. This is a very visual task and isn't necessary. Squeeze a pea-sized amount onto the child's finger. Then, using the hand over hand method, move their finger into their mouth and rub the paste onto their front teeth. Hand the child the brush, then encourage it into their mouth and let them explore the brush and their own teeth.

If the child is reluctant, try exploring the model of human teeth and brushing those teeth instead.

If in doubt, refer to 3.09, 'Tooth brushing' (pages 33–35), for guidance on developing skills.

Now have fun, singing along with 'This Is the Way We Brush Our Teeth'.

THINGS TO CONSIDER

It is important you make this activity as much fun as it can be! A child needs to understand that it is something that needs to be done twice a day, and particularly before bed. Children with a vision impairment cannot acquire this skill through observation or incidental learning, and therefore will need time and patience to build it into their daily routine. It is worth trying hard to find a flavour of toothpaste your child likes: if the taste is an issue, it could become a major problem.

Watch out your child does not push the brush too far to the back of his mouth. Aside from potentially causing injury, this can make him gag, and might put him off the whole process.

Small children should not use adult-sized toothbrushes.

Busy Bag 12
Learn to skip

RESOURCES

An adult, one or more children (aged five and above, depending on physical maturity), a level space and a skipping rope.

CHOOSE YOUR ROPE

When we were children, our skipping ropes were made out of old washing lines cut to size. These days, you can pay as much or as little as you want for one – they are available in toy shops, sports shops and even pound shops. Make sure the rope is flexible enough; better quality ropes will have bearings in the handles. If your child has some useful vision, choose the colour that she sees best. You can even buy light-up ropes!

Just make sure it is the right size for your child. Most children will adjust. However, to measure the optimum size, stand on the centre of the rope, and it should reach up to the sternum (or the handles to reach to under the armpits). If the rope is too long, it will tangle. Remember that elite sportspeople, including boxers, skip every day as part of their daily training regime. It is far from being just for girls!

BENEFITS OF SKIPPING

Skipping aids developmental skills that children need to be successful in school – bilateral coordination, motor planning, hand–eye coordination, jumping, strength and endurance (and jumping is often a benchmark in PE). Skipping can be a great solitary activity or provide opportunities for socialisation.

Learn skipping

WHERE TO START

What is the best way to help your child learn how to skip? It may take time, so don't rush the stages. Make it fun.

The Americans call skipping 'jumping rope'. This may be a better way of explaining it to a child with vision impairment. Introduce the child to the rope and handles, then lie the rope on the floor. Let the child feel with their feet and experiment stepping on, stepping over and then jumping over the rope. the height of the jump is not important – just enough is perfect. Are we jumping yet? Does your child need more reassurance? Try holding one hand and saying 'Jump!'

Next, give the child the skipping rope. Encourage her to locate and hold the handles, and then stand on the rope and jump off.

See if your child can hold both handles in one hand, with the looped rope touching the floor. Use the hand she prefers and encourage her to swing the rope round and round in circles. Keep her arm out for now, and make sure the rope doesn't hit her. Maybe do it together, and try to encourage the addition of a little jump as the rope grounds. Listen for the 'slap' as it grounds. Add a song or skipping game rhyme. This will help develop rhythm and make it all more fun.

Next, get her to hold the handles and place the jump rope behind her body. Then swing the jump rope gently over to the front and then to the back. Practise this several times, just swinging the rope from the front to back. Now swing the jump rope to the front and let it stay on the ground. Keep the rope still and jump over it. The loop is now complete! Practise this step several times. This is the point where it helps if the rope is a colour that she can see against the floor. However, if not, get her to listen for the little 'slap' as the rope hits the floor.

Learn skipping

READY, STEADY, SKIP!

Now it's time to put it all together. Get your child to swing the jump rope from the back to the front of her body and, when it gets close to her feet, say 'JUMP!' It takes practice to get the timing just right.

Adding a song or rhyme will help with timing and coordination. Anything will do, but a few skipping rhymes are suggested below. Some children find that counting helps. Challenge her to increase the number of successful jumps without stopping. Once your child gets the hang of this, she has a source of independent entertainment, as well as the opportunity to develop a range of skills.

Encourage jumping on the toes. When a child is skipping proficiently, the heels should not touch the ground. The higher she jumps, the more difficult the timing will be. As she progresses, don't encourage too much arm movement. Good skipping depends on a wrist movement, rather than a whole-arm movement.

Bobby Shaftoe

Bobby Shaftoe went to sea,
Silver buckles on his knee,
He'll come back to marry me,
Bonny Bobby Shaftoe.

Bobby Shaftoe's bright and fair,
Combing down his yellow hair,
He's my love forever more,
Bonny Bobby Shaftoe.

Bobby Shaftoe went to sea,
Silver buckles on his knee,
He'll come back to marry me,
Bonny Bobby Shaftoe,
How many days until he comes back?
[1, 2, 3 count until someone misses]

One, Two, Buckle My Shoe

One two, buckle my shoe,
Three four, close the door,
Five six, pick up sticks,
Seven eight, shut the gate,
Nine ten, start again.

Learn skipping

All in together girls [boys],
All out together girls [boys],
It's fine weather girls [boys,]
When it's your birthday, please jump out,
1, 2, 3, 4, 5, 6, 7, 8, 9, 10, 11, 12, 13, 14, …

All in together girls,
It's fine weather girls,
When is your birthday, please jump in,
[now really fast]
January, February, March, April, May, June, July, August, September, October,
November, December.

Teddy bear, teddy bear, turn around,
Teddy bear, teddy bear, touch the ground,
Teddy bear, teddy bear, show your shoe,
Teddy bear, teddy bear, that will do!
Teddy bear, teddy bear, go upstairs,
Teddy bear, teddy bear, say your prayers,
Teddy bear, teddy bear, turn out the lights,
Teddy bear, teddy bear, say good night!

[The children jump rope while they sing this rhyme. They act out the actions as the words come up in the rhyme. For example, when the rhyme says 'go upstairs', the child pretends to climb the stairs.]

Find lots more ideas on YouTube.

Busy Bag 13a
Tying shoelaces part 1

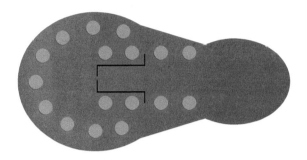

RESOURCES

Shoelace with aglet (plastic cover over the end of the lace), shoelace frame or lacing card, hole punch, laminator.

DIRECTIONS

Laminate the shoelace frame (this gives it durability), then make eyelet holes using a hole punch.

Spend time encouraging your child to weave the lace in and out from one end of the frame to the other. At this stage, this is the main target, as it will build the dexterity necessary for fastening laces. There is no hurry to progress. This activity requires a great deal of repetition and patience – from both of you.

As you do your own shoelaces, get your child to put their hands on top of yours. This allows them to 'watch' you go through the actions, and helps them get a feel for the motions they will be using. Make sure they sit next to you, rather than facing you. This way, they can get used to how the actions feel from the correct perspective. Keep the tying method consistent, as there are a variety of ways to tie shoelaces.

Once the child is ready to move on from just 'watching' you tie laces, make sure you continue to support them from behind. Start by aiming to complete the first crossover and the first knot. Let them take the lead, with you gently correcting movements and guiding when necessary. As they go through the motions, get them to explain what they're doing with each movement.

Finish each attempt with positive feedback.

THINGS TO CONSIDER

It is not easy learning to tie shoelaces, and nor is teaching it. This is a complex skill that will take time to master.

Vision impaired children may have problems with hand–eye coordination. They can get confused by all the criss-crossing and looping of laces, and their visual system suddenly cannot distinguish between one lace and the other.

Stock up with laces that look and feel different. Help your child look for different colours and textures. This will help when you move onto the next stage – Busy Bag 13b: Tying shoelaces part 2 (pages 127–129).

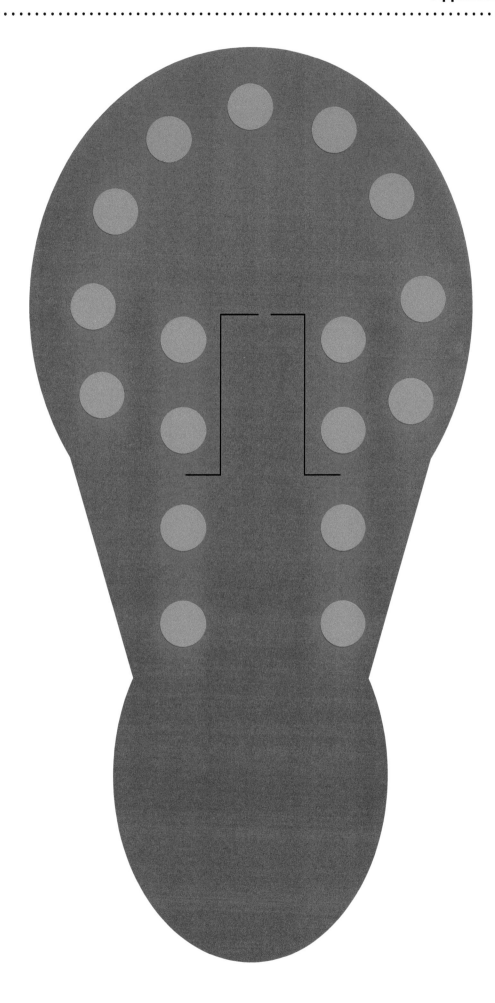

Busy Bag 13b
Tying shoelaces part 2

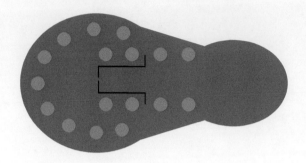

RESOURCES

Shoelace (with aglet), shoelace frame (or lacing card) from Busy Bag 13a: Tying shoelaces part 1 (page 127); real shoe and laces (once the skill is mastered).

DIRECTIONS

If you have not already done lacing and threading, start with Busy Bag 13a: Tying shoelaces part 1 (pages 125–127).

Make sure that the shoe or shoelace frame is facing away from your child. Initially, fasten together laces with different colour and texture. This helps the child identify which lace is which (see right). It is often also helpful to choose laces that contrast with the shoe.

Keep the tying method consistent. There is no single way to tie shoelaces. Each method starts with making an 'X' and then a knot. Have your child master these first two steps before moving on. Sometimes this is a good place to stop and consolidate the skills.

The bunny ears (or chocolate bow) method uses the same knot twice. Only move onto the second knot when the first knot is secure.

Make two loops (or 'bunny ears'). Be sure the child holds them close to the first knot and leaves a long tail at both ends. Then the child needs to cross the loops over and repeat the first knot.

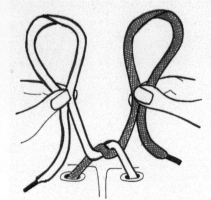

Bunny Ears or Chocolate Box Bow

If using the more traditional single loop tying method, a rhyme or story can help your child remember the steps. One of the best known and simple ways to remember this is 'Loop, swoop and pull'.

Alternatively try making an 'X'. Pull the top lace through, then pull it tight.

Make one loop, holding it tight at the bottom. This loop is a 'tree'. The other lace is going to be a 'bunny'. The 'bunny' runs around the 'tree' and goes into his 'hole'. And then you pull the loops tight – voilà!

Follow this link to find some shoe-tying videos: https://theinspiredtreehouse.com/child-development-teaching-kids-how-to-tie-their-shoes/

THINGS TO CONSIDER

If you are demonstrating, or working hand over hand, make sure the child is sitting next to you or facing forwards in front of you. This way, they can get used to how the actions feel from the correct perspective. However, if they sit facing you, they will have to mirror the actions (which can be much more difficult).

Learning to tie laces is definitely not easy, nor is it an easy skill to teach.

Children with a visual impairment may have problems linking what their eyes are seeing and what their hands are doing – essentially, hand–eye coordination. They become easily confused by all the criss-crossing and looping of laces, and their visual system suddenly cannot distinguish one lace from the other. This is why different coloured or different textured laces may help.

For children with no useful vision, use one rounded lace and one flat lace.

Children who struggle to control the 'bunny ears' may benefit from trying first with pipe cleaners or wired ribbon. This helps keep the 'bunny ears' upright.

Busy Bag 14
Messy play

RESOURCES

Jelly* (or spaghetti, or mashed potato – homemade or instant), small toys (like Lego®) or coloured sweets (Smarties or M&M's); choose things that will wash easily or (better still) can go in the dishwasher!

*You can use any sort of jelly (including vegetarian jelly). Glitter jelly is lovely if your child has useful vision.

DIRECTIONS

Make up the jelly as directed on the packaging. Then leave to set slightly. Also consider mashed potato or spaghetti for a very different, edible texture experience. If your jelly has a strong colour, you can add squirty cream for a contrast and a different sensation.

Add in your preferred clean objects/toys (Lego®, shapes, animals) or foodstuffs (Smarties, fruit) or anything that particularly interests your child. Don't choose anything that will dissolve in the jelly.

Leave the jelly to set fully in the fridge. Then play 'Hunting for the Treasure' together.

REMEMBER

➢ To reduce the risk of choking, supervise your child at all times.

➢ Don't mix edible and non-edible contents unless you are sure your child will recognise the difference.

➢ If using grapes, remember to cut them in half lengthways.

➢ If your child is not keen to engage, try the **hand under hand** technique (see next page).

THINGS TO CONSIDER

This fun activity introduces a variety of textures and consistencies. It also helps the child learn more about the world around them and develops the sense of touch. Messy play can be a great multi-sensory experience.

For some children with a visual impairment, however, it can also prove challenging. Some children may have issues around using touch to explore, and certain textures may trigger anxieties or a reluctance to participate. The child may be hypersensitive to some textures and may be sensory avoidant (formerly known as tactile defensive). Others simply don't like messy activities! For some children, messy play may always be a challenge. However, by trying to understand the activity from the child's perspective, and by being patient and giving them lots of time, they may learn to experience messy play as a fun activity rather than an ordeal.

HAND UNDER HAND METHOD

Some children are resistant to trying new activities. They may pull their hands away and won't want to touch. But, if they are never encouraged to try new things, they may not ever expand their understanding and interest in the world around them.

When you use the hand under hand technique, your hands perform the activity while your child's hands rest on top of yours. In this way, they can feel what your hands are doing. If their palms are on your hands, the child will be able to focus on feeling the movements of your hands. Your child will get tactile feedback in this way and may feel more comfortable and in control, as they can freely remove their hands (if that is what they want to do). If there is something that your child particularly likes, this may help them overcome their reluctance.

Remember: describe what you are doing with your hands as you perform the activity.

Appendix 2:
Activity Sheets

These can be used by a child to develop skills from the book. Alternatively, a professional may choose to print activities out and send them home for repetition. Each Activity Sheet outlines the resources you need and provides instructions.

Activity Sheet 1
I can fasten 1

Name .... Date ....

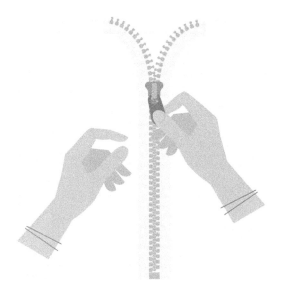

 Zip

 Button

Velcro® Laces

Activity Sheet 2
I can fasten 2

Name .... Date ....

 **Belt**

Watch

 **Necklace clasp**

Purse popper

Shoelaces

Open-ended zip

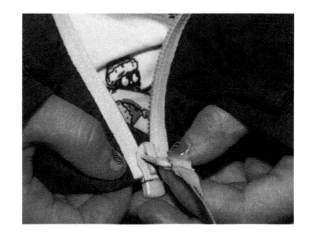

Activity Sheet 3
I can look after my clothes

Name ....   Date ....

I can fold clothes

I can hang clothes on hangers

I can hang my coat up

I can put my clothes where I can find them

I can put my shoes on the correct feet

I can clean my glasses

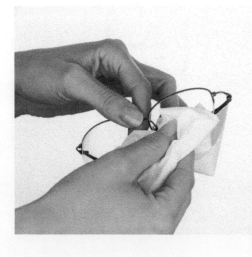

Activity Sheet 4
Hand-washing

These are the steps for washing your hands. Cut them out and stick them in the correct order on a blank sheet of paper.

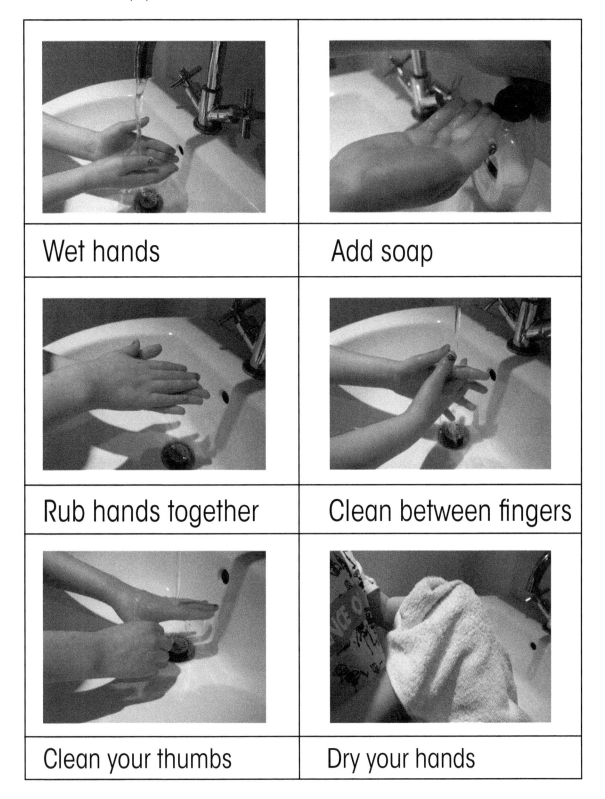

Wet hands	Add soap
Rub hands together	Clean between fingers
Clean your thumbs	Dry your hands

Activity Sheet 5
Using scissors

Use the following five sheets (Activity Sheets 5a–5e) for cutting practice.

The lines are thick enough to be visible to a child with some useful vision. The pages will also copy well onto swell paper if the line is not visible. As an alternative to swell paper, you can go over the lines with Wikki Stix®, which are reusable.

if a child does not have useful vision, using scissors is difficult. You may need to consider using scissors that allow the adult to support cutting.

The thick lines can be used for writing, as well as cutting practice.

Remember: Early writing is always quite large. Give your child a thick pen – like the Berol broad – so he can see his writing.

Activity Sheet 5a

Activity Sheet 5b

Wavy line

Activity Sheet 5c

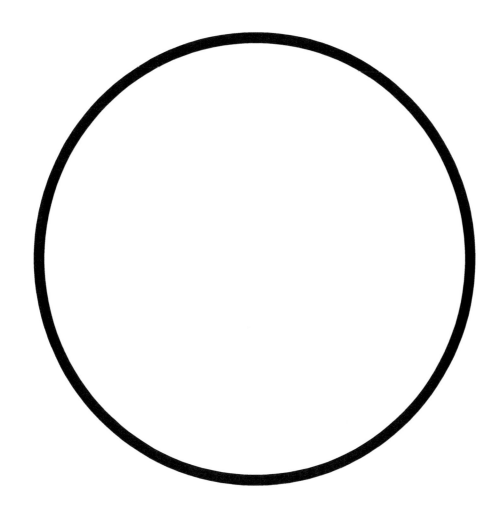

Circle

Activity Sheet 5d

Rectangle

Activity Sheet 5e
Paper Chinese lantern instructions

This paper Chinese lantern is easy to make, looks great and provides useful cutting practice. Choose a paper colour that the child can see well. Children with severe sight impairment can achieve this task by using swell paper to produce raised lines. You can use Wikki Stix®, but the children may need help to hold them in place.

1. Start with a rectangular sheet of paper or card. Cut a strip of paper from the long edge of the paper – about 2.5 cm (1 in) width. This will be used as the handle of the lantern.

2. Fold the paper in half lengthwise. Cut strips crosswise: cut from the folded edge towards the top, following the lines to keep straight. Be careful to keep the strips connected, and do not cut to the edge of the paper. You can put a piece of Blu Tack® (or similar) to indicate when to stop.

3. Unfold the paper.

4. Loop the paper around to form a tube, putting the visible lines inside. Join the short ends of the paper together with tape, staples or glue.

5. Attach the handle you made in step 1 (using staple, glue, sticky tape).

6. You can make a number of lanterns and string them all together. This gives an opportunity for repetition and also to introduce a variety of different colours.

7. Decorate the lanterns as desired.

Activity Sheet 6
Money, not money

Name ....   Date ....

Separate money from other things.

As a variation, you could replace the circles with pots or a sorting tray.

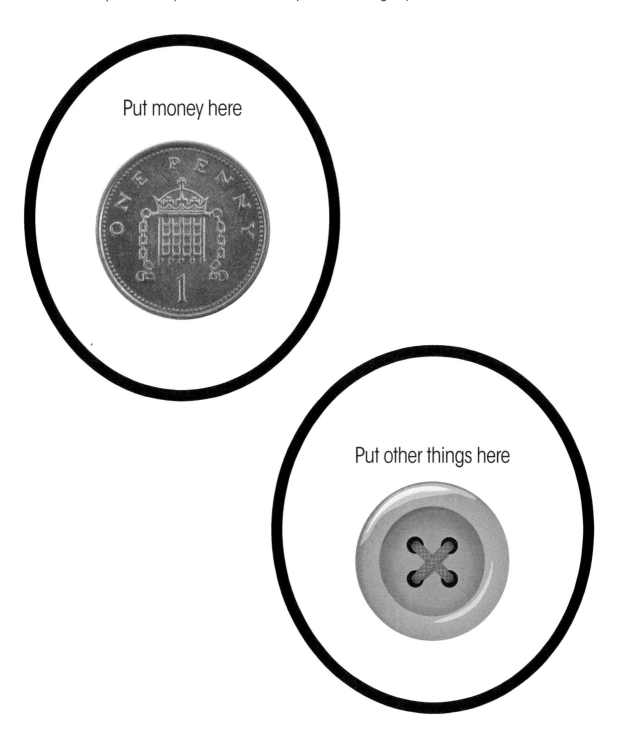

Put money here

Put other things here

Activity Sheet 7
1p sum sheet

Name .... Date ....

1p   +   1p   =

1p   +   1p   +   1p   =

1p   +   1p   +   1p   +   1p   =

Activity Sheet 8
2p sum sheet

Name .... Date ....

2p   +   1p   =

2p   +   1p   +   1p   =

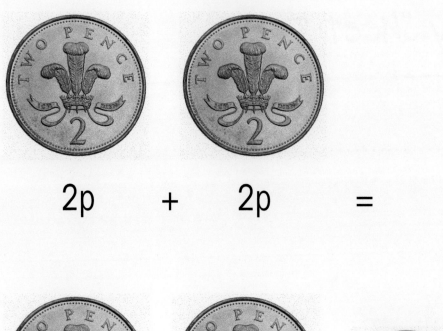

2p   +   2p   =

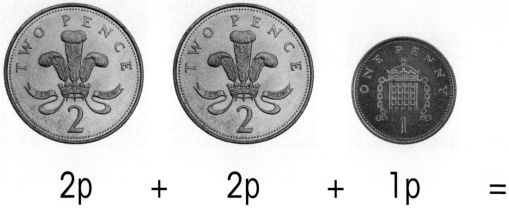

2p   +   2p   +   1p   =

Activity Sheet 9
Coin identification

Name .... Date ....

Place the matching coin in the box or write down the correct amount.

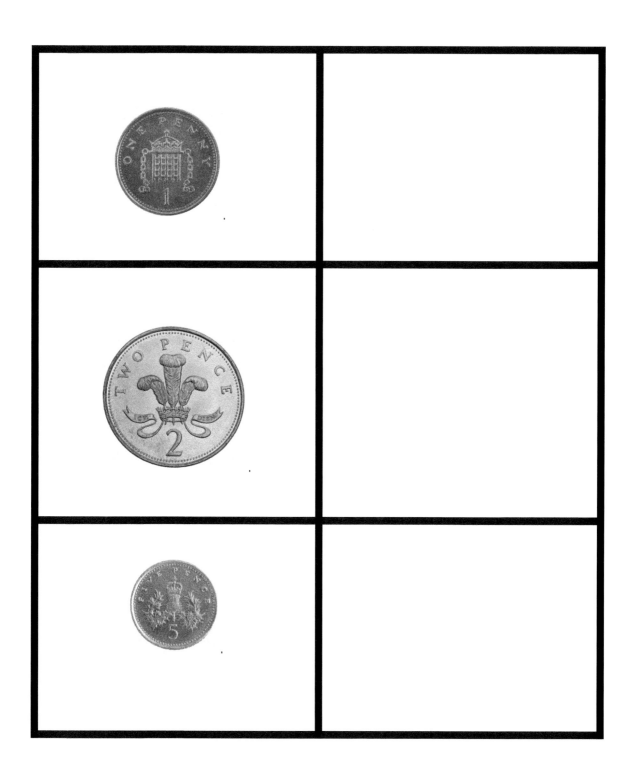

153

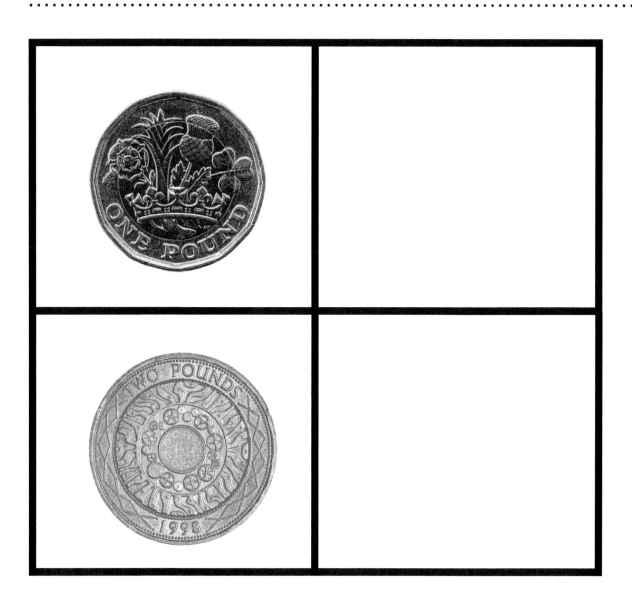

Activity Sheet 10
Clock face

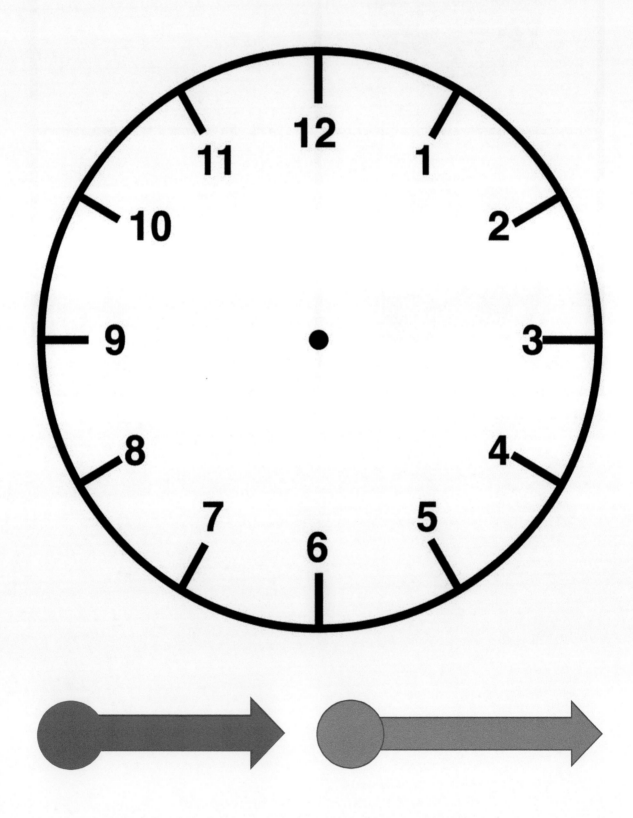

Activity Sheet 10
Clock face

155

Print the clock face and hands onto some card.

Cut out the clock and hands and fix the hands onto the clock with a split pin.

Make sure you leave enough 'play' in the split pin so the hands can move easily.

To make it tactile, put one dot on the 1, 2, 4, 5, 7, 8, 10 and 11, and two dots on the 3, 6, 9 and 12.

Activity Sheet 11
My first body parts

Head
Eyes
Ears
Mouth
Nose
Hands
Fingers
Feet
Toes
Tummy
Bottom
Arm
Leg

The child can either write out these body part words in the boxes provided, or cut and paste them into the boxes.

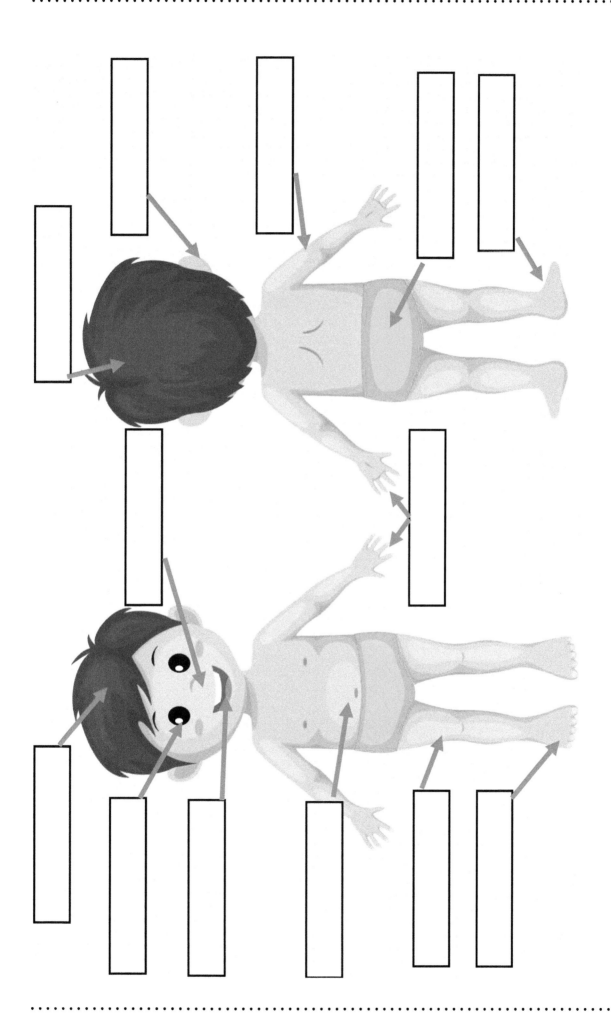

Activity Sheet 12
Motor scavenger hunt

Find something:

◯ to climb up

◯ to slide down

◯ to roll over

◯ to climb over

◯ to crawl under

◯ to jump off

◯ to pick up

You can either do this in your own garden or at the park. Add or remove categories to suit your child and the location.

If your child wants to splash in water, they'll need wellies. However, they are difficult to climb in and only give limited feedback through the feet, so choose other footwear (if possible).

You may like to combine this with Activity Sheet 13: Sensory scavenger hunt.

Consider adding:

- ➢ to run on
- ➢ to balance on
- ➢ big to hug

- ➢ to hop on
- ➢ to sit on
- ➢ high to stretch up to

(like a tree)

Activity Sheet 13
Sensory scavenger hunt

Find something:

 hard

 soft

 smooth

 rough

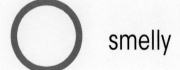 squishy

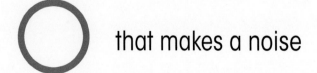 smelly

 that makes a noise

You can either do this in your own garden or at the park. Add or remove categories to suit your child and the location.

If your child wants to splash in water, they'll need wellies. However, they are difficult to climb in and only give limited feedback through the feet, so choose other footwear (if possible).

You may like to combine this with Activity Sheet 12: Motor scavenger hunt.

Consider adding:

- wet
- cold
- crunchy
- dry
- warm
- slippy

Appendices

· ·

Activity Sheet 14
Post a letter

Introduce the postal system by watching or reading a Postman Pat story with your child. Show her where letters arrive at home. When you go out on the Mobility adventure walk (Busy Bag 7), try to find a postbox and show her where letters get posted.

Work together to produce a letter or card that your child can post to herself. A standard postcard will be too small, so use the postcard supplied overleaf or use a piece of A4 card or Braille paper.

Even if your child cannot read, include some words in the letter, but make it more exciting by decorating it with pictures, colours or different textures. It is important for her to understand that post is a way of communicating with others. Explain the difference between postal mail and email.

Take this opportunity to discuss your address. Children often don't understand the term 'address', so you may have to explain that an address is the place where you live. Whenever you can, get your child to rehearse her address.

Show her where to write the address and where the stamp goes. Even if your child qualifies to use the Articles for the Blind (www.royalmail.com/sending/articles-blind), do this, so she understands the system.

When your letter is ready, go to the postbox. Let your child post the letter into the box and listen to the sound it makes when it lands inside. If you can time your visit with a postal collection, the delivery worker may let her feel the open door and sack when they remove the mail. If not, let her explore, feeling where the key fits in the door.

The difficult bit is waiting for the letter to arrive. Articles for the Blind post travels first class, so it should arrive within a day or so. If you are using a stamp, make sure it is first class – at least the first time. If your item is large, you may need a special large letter stamp.

Repeat the exercise. This time, send a letter to a friend or relative, who will write back to your child.

· ·

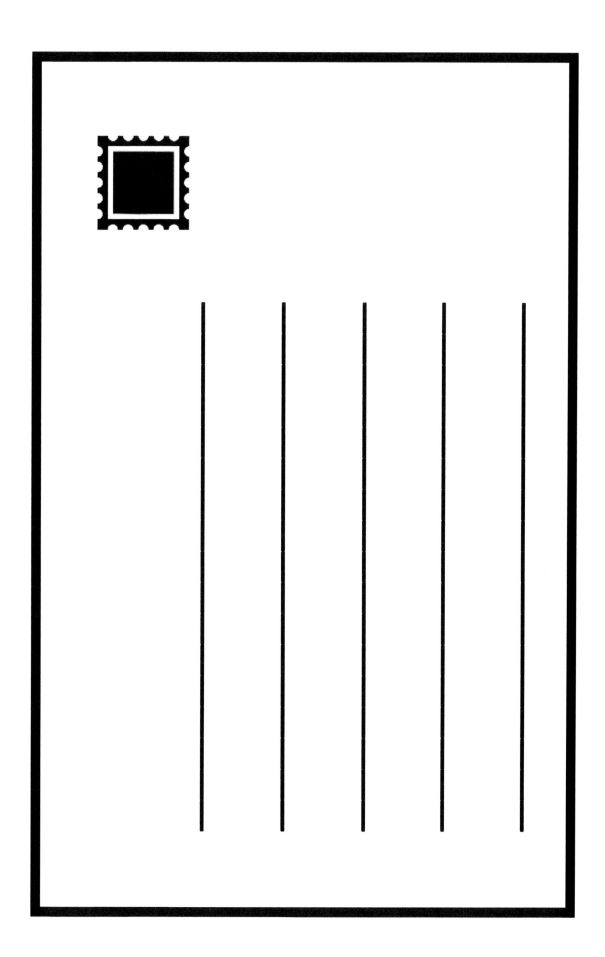

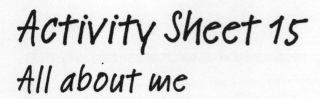

Activity Sheet 15
All about me

Remember: It's more important to talk the information through than for the child to write anything down.

My name is:

....

Here is a photo of me:

(stick your photo here or make a tactile image)

My school/nursery is called:

....

....

I live at:

....

....

....

This is my address.

I live with:

....

....

....

More about my family:

(include names)

....

....

....

....

Things I like doing:

(write, or stick pictures in)

....

....

....

....

....

My favourite foods:

(write, or stick pictures in)

....

....

....

....

Activity Sheet 16
Urban trail

Name ....

Tick the boxes as you find things.

A postbox

It is made of

_____

I have found a streetlight.

It is made of_____.

I have found a hedge.

I have found a kerb.

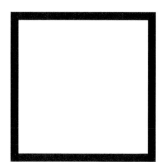

I must stay on the pavement to keep safe.

I have found a bin.

It is made of_____.

What goes in the bin?

How many
different
bollards can
you find?

_____

The bollards are
made of

_____.

I have
found
a bus
shelter.

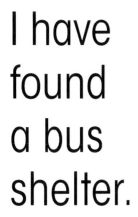

Can you hear the echo?

I can find my home.

I can identify it by

_____.

Appendix 3: Handouts

These Handouts are intended to support learning with either supplementary information or a precis of the main text. A professional may choose to print Handouts and send them home to parents or carers to introduce an activity or topic. Each Handout covers a different topic. It outlines any resources you may need and provides instructions. All the Handouts relate to specific sections or themes from the book.

Handout 1
Cardboard boxes

Never underestimate the value of a cardboard box!

Look for sturdy varieties, but do avoid those with big staples.

Think of a baby's excitement pulling the wrapping off a Christmas present, and how disappointed parents are when the gift is cast aside in favour of the box and wrapping paper! This is how exciting a box can be to a child!

The inside of a cardboard box is cosy. Your child can reach the sides, he is no longer in an open space and he can begin to figure out how he fits in that space. Inside is warm and smooth, and if the box is big enough it may even echo a little.

You can play Hide and Seek, or Peekaboo. It is normal for young children to hide in the same place repeatedly. You are learning 'now you see me, now you don't'. This is a complex notion for severely sight impaired children, who can forget that other people can see them.

The box can be a car, a train, a house, whatever your child wants… There is no need to decorate it, but add descriptive images and fun through onomatopoeia – 'Brrmmm, brrmmm' or 'Shooosh, shoosh'. 'Clickety-clack' is a personal favourite!

If he wants to do something more artistic, let him colour the inside of the box with crayons or pens. Writing on a vertical surface uses different muscles, and strengthens the neck and shoulders. It also gives a completely different perception of things, viewing everything from a different angle.

If your child is feeling boisterous, let him kick in the sides. Although probably irritating to parents, this helps develop proprioception and teaches him about force and resistance. The bits may be useful for other activities, but in the end the box can always be recycled!

Handout 2
Homemade playdough

INGREDIENTS

(This makes one ball of dough.)

➤ 8 tablespoons plain flour

➤ 2 tablespoons salt

➤ 4 tablespoons water

➤ 1 tablespoons vegetable oil

➤ Food colouring

Get your child involved from the outset. Mixing and kneading are great fun, and also build up hand strength.

Mix the flour and salt in a large bowl. In a separate bowl, mix together the water, the oil and a few drops of food colouring. (Choose a colour that is more visible or attractive to your child, and select a contrasting board to work on.)

Pour the coloured water into the flour mix and bring together with a spoon.

Sprinkle the cooking board a with a little flour and turn out the mixture. Knead together to make a smooth, pliable dough. Add some extra food colouring if it's not colourful enough.

Store the dough in a plastic sandwich bag (remember to squeeze out the air) and put it in the fridge to keep it fresh. As the volume is relatively small, you can make a couple of playdough batches in different colours.

Note: Whilst this recipe is edible, eating it is not recommended!

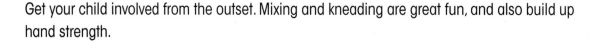

Gluten-free playdough

INGREDIENTS

(This makes a large tub of dough.)

- 230 g (8 oz) rice flour

- 230 g (8 oz) cornflour

- 230 g (8 oz) salt

- 4 teaspoons cream of tartar

- 2 cups water

- 2 tablespoons vegetable oil

- Food colouring

Place all ingredients into a saucepan.

Cook over a low heat for about 5 minutes. Stir all the time, until the mixture thickens. (Remember to choose a food colouring that is more visible or attractive to your child, and select a contrasting board to work on.)

Remove the saucepan from the heat, tip the mixture onto the board and knead it to remove any lumps. This is the point when your child can join in! Mixing and kneading are great fun, and they also build up hand strength.

Roll into a large ball and store in air-tight container.

Note: Although edible, and gluten free, eating this dough is not recommended!

Gluten-free playdough

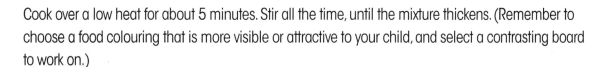

Handout 3
How to make gloop

YOU WILL NEED

➢ A tray with deep sides

➢ Cornflour

➢ Water

Cover all surfaces and your children, as this activity gets messy!

Pour some cornflour into a large tray.

Slowly pour in some cold water. You will need to play about with how much water to add. You want it to be thin enough to move with your hands, but not watery.

Now the fun begins. Get your hands in and play with the gloop. It really is magical, as you can pick up chunks that are almost solid... and then they fall, like water, back into the mixture!

To make the gloop more visible, you can add glitter or food colouring to the mixture.

Note: Whilst the gloop is edible, and gluten free, eating it is not recommended!

Handout 4
Dressing tricks and tips

➢ It is often faster and easier to dress your child rather than letting him have a go. Therefore, you may have to allocate times when you let him dress himself, probably when you are under no time pressure. Making a big fuss when he does anything for himself will boost his confidence and self-esteem.

➢ Dressing requires a range of movement and a degree of muscle strength and coordination. Your child will also need a degree of balance and fine motor skills.

➢ To prepare for dressing skills, look for tasks and games that develop motor skills, particularly those around fine motor hand skills. Mix and match activities.

➢ Describe actions and parts of the body as you help your child to dress. Don't worry too much about right and left – that will come later. Be consistent: always get him to put the same clothes on in the same way.

➢ Velcro® is great, and a good starting point. However, new Velcro® sometimes needs a great deal of force to separate the two sides, or as it ages it can get so clogged with fluff that it no longer grips. Use a fine-toothed comb to tease the threads out.

➢ Big buttons are easier than small buttons, as long as the buttonholes are large enough. Colour-contrast button and material for practice. If you have a crafty friend or relative, see if they can create a button fastening activity. This one (right) is made from strips of felt with contrasting buttons.

➢ A small button in the inside top back of clothing helps ensure clothes are the right way up and right way round. Label locations are not reliable enough. Some labels can pose a problem to children with sensory issues, so a degree of lateral thinking may be required.

➢ Use a zip pull to make it easier for the child to slide the zip up or down. You can buy them quite cheaply online or you can buy character ones to engage the child. Alternatively, you can just loop a hair bobble through.

➢ For teaching purposes, look for a bold contrast between zip teeth and the fabric of the zip. You can buy zips of different colours and mix and match. This will make both the teeth and process more visible. Bigger zips are easier and to manipulate and to learn how to use.

➢ Suggest appropriate clothing, such as joggers or elasticated shorts. Opt for clothing items that are stretchy and/or not too tight.

➢ Start off sitting down to pull joggers on, as balancing on one leg makes the process much more difficult. Tie in undressing with potty training or toileting skills.

➢ When your child grows out of his coat, try to avoid buying one that is significantly different, as this may require a new skillset.

➢ Hoods on coats provide a great starting point. A furry hood, or a button inside, helps the child know the coat is the right way up.

➢ Suggest that your child's school or nursery make his coat peg easily accessible (perhaps on the end of the row). Also, request bright, bold or tactile signage to identify the peg. Make a similar suggestion for their locker position.

➢ As he progresses, encourage him to be systematic about where he puts his clothing when he takes it off. A chair is a really good place. Once he starts dressing himself more, place his clothes on the chair in the order he needs to put them on.

➢ If he has useful vision, he may find it helpful to have a visual timetable showing the order of dressing.

➢ Shoelaces are a difficult skill for all children to acquire. Therefore, learning this is best left until other dressing skills are secure. However, the prerequisite skills – like developing the pincer grip and threading – can be introduced with a view to tying laces when your child is ready.

➢ There is always more than one way to do something!

Handout 5
This Is the Way We Brush Our Teeth

(To the tune of 'Here We Go Round the Mulberry Bush')

This is the way we brush our teeth, brush our teeth, brush our teeth,

This is the way we brush our teeth, early in the morning (or 'on our way to bed').

This is the way we brush our teeth, toothpaste on, toothpaste on,

This is the way we brush our teeth, a pea-sized blob of toothpaste.

This is the way we brush our teeth, round and round, round and round,

This is the way we brush our teeth, round and round in circles.

This is the way we brush our teeth, front and back, front and back,

This is the way we brush our teeth, till they're clean and sparkly.

This is the way we brush our teeth, two minutes long, two minutes long,

This is the way we brush our teeth, let's hum it through again.

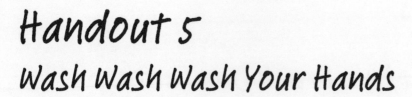

Handout 5
Wash Wash Wash Your Hands

(To the tune of 'Row, Row, Row Your Boat')

Wash, wash, wash your hands,

To get them very clean,

Soap them up and scrub and rub,

Germs are very mean.

Wash, wash, wash your hands,

Let's all sing this twice,

Soap them up and scrub and rub,

Being clean is really nice!

Handout 6
Supporting cold pouring

Using a liquid level indicator

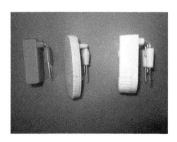

Usually, habilitation specialists will introduce your child to the range of liquid level indicators, and advise on the most suitable one. However, each local authority is different.

Liquid level indicators are available from the RNIB (www.rnib.org.uk/) and Cobolt Systems Ltd (www.cobolt.co.uk/). All make a noise to indicate that the liquid is approaching the top of the cup, and a different warning noise to indicate that you should stop pouring.

Vibrating sensors are available for those who have hearing problems. Different indicators make different noises, and some children may prefer one to another. The metal sensors hang inside the cup, and the battery and sound pack on the outside.

Children should always begin with cold pouring, and must not progress to hot drinks until competent with cold liquids. This way, the techniques for both are learned without the risks that come with hot water. Aside from the child's competence, remember that kettles (and other vessels that hold hot water) are heavy.

Although they may be safe with cold drinks, children should be discouraged from using fingers to check the height of the liquid or, initially, even holding the cup. This practice will stand them in good stead when they do move onto hot pouring.

Use a mug to start with, as they are more stable than glasses or plastic beakers. Pour onto a high-sided tray, to catch any spills. This also keeps all items together and reduces the risk of scalds later when pouring hot liquids.

If your child has some useful vision, make sure there is good contrast between the cup, tray or worksurface – and, if possible, the colour of the liquid to be poured.

Avoid very big squash bottles, as they are often too heavy for a small child. Instead, use smaller squash bottles (or transfer liquids into a sports bottle), to help the child maximise control of pouring. This is particularly useful for small hands. It slows the flow down and also reduces spillage if the bottle is knocked over.

Handout 7
Make your own blow football game

You will need

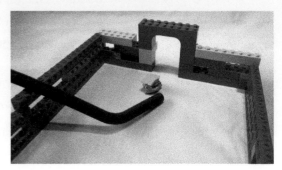

➢ Building blocks (Duplo®, Lego® or Mega Bloks®)

➢ Bendy straws

➢ Ping pong ball (bright colour)

This great blow football game is easy to build with your child – and playing it provides hours of fun! Work together to build the stadium and goals. The sides keep the ball contained and make the game easier for a low vision child. Let him choose building block colours that he sees well, and get him to identify the colours. Make sure the goals contrast well and are big enough for the ball to pass through. To give greater firepower, tape two straws together.

Collect a block and build it into a score tower. Agree your own rules beforehand (for example, the first person to five wins, or poking the ball instead of blowing results in a penalty). It can be as simple of complicated as you wish. Every time you score, add a block to your score tower. No ping pong ball? Try screwed-up paper or even a cotton ball. When you choose the ping pong ball, make sure its colour contrasts with the pitch.

As well as being great fun, this game helps develop scanning and tracking, counting and manual dexterity. It will also help develop children's resilience, as they learn they can't win every time. The game promotes self-regulation, as well, rehearsing appropriate responses to winning and losing. It is also particularly good for developing oral motor skills – the skills that help move food round the mouth for effective chewing and swallowing.

Not quite sure where to start? Check out this Lego® family video on YouTube: https://youtu.be/PQ-lzZqlhOY

Handout 8
10 simple ways to work on balance skills

These activities aim to improve your child with visual impairment's balance, coordination, core stability and foot placement.

1. With your child, walk up and down **single steps or kerbs**. Each time you take a step, you are balancing on one foot, so make sure the step height is not too great for a small child. You can support him, if necessary, by holding hands. Establish secure movement on up and down steps before your child progresses to unsupported movement.

2. **Sit and ride toys**. Start your child on wider, solid-wheelbase toys. Move on to tricycles, which are reasonably stable, but pedalling and steering them requires considerable coordination. Watch out for oversteer! Then progress to a balance bike – a task that requires considerable postural control and balance.

3. **Ride a scooter**. Start your child on a three-wheeled scooter, as they are more stable (and therefore easier to ride) than two-wheeled ones.

4. With your child, **walk on uneven terrain**: grass, rocks or dirt. Wet, thick mud is very challenging, though. If sensory issues permit, encourage your child to walk barefoot on grass and wet and dry sand (wet sand creates the most resistance). Kick through the leaves in autumn.

5. Play a **game of football** together. This requires him to stand on one foot to kick the ball. Swinging his active leg provides further challenges to stability. To start with, choose a large, high-visibility or audible ball.

6. Play **'Find Me' or 'Follow the Leader'** together. Practise walking fast, slow, backwards and sideways, hopping on one leg and skipping. Alternate with 'Traffic Lights', 'Stop-Go', etc. Progress to 'Pirates' or 'Simon Says'.

7. **Walk the tightrope.** Get your child to walk heel to toe along any visible or tactile line. Or play 'Cross the Rickety Bridge' (this can be a low-level beam or even a rope). You can make the

game entertaining by having a 'crocodile' in the water! Progress to stepping stones. Use 'Three Billy Goats Gruff' as a variation.

8. Try **putting trousers or joggers on while standing**. It's a real challenge standing on one foot while putting the other leg into a pair of trousers!

9. Look for **gross motor activities at the park**, particularly those that encourage rocking and swaying.

10. Encourage your child to use **portable play equipment**: trampolines, wobble boards, Gymnic Rody horse, etc.

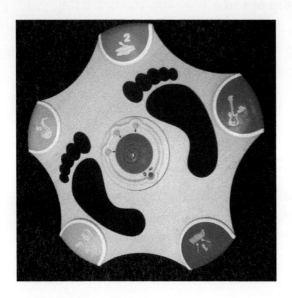

Handout 9
Stomp and catch/joey jump

This activity is an inexpensive way for your child with a vision impairment to keep themselves occupied and also improve their catching skills. The object is for the child to locate and stamp on the end of the board, flicking the beanbag or Koosh ball up towards them to catch. It also improves foot– and hand–eye coordination. It requires some basic equipment and a few DIY skills. However, if DIY is not your thing, you can buy one of these online and adapt the activity to make it easier for your child:

www.ypo.co.uk/product/detail/Sports/General-Play/803968

www.sportsdirectoryuk.co.uk/product/joey_jump_bean_bag_game

YOU WILL NEED

➤ Piece of board around 70 cm x 10 cm (28 in x 4 in)

➤ Plastic tubing 8–10 cm (3–4 in) long, approx. 5 cm (2 in) diameter

➤ Beanbag or Koosh ball

➤ Extra-strong adhesive

➤ *Optional*: paint, sandpaper

Round and sand the edges of the board. If you want to paint it, choose a strong colour that your child may be able to see and that provides a contrast with the surface. Glue the tubing onto the base about 15 cm (6 in) away from the end. You can add a couple of screws if you wish. Allow the glue to set.

At the opposite end of the board, add lines of glue. This is to stop the beanbags sliding down the board. (Alternatively, you can glue some sandpaper onto the top surface.)

Balls are much more likely to slide down the board and are also more difficult to catch. Koosh balls or beanbags are preferable, as these 'die' in the hand. You may wish to make your own

beanbags. Recycle old material or buy fat squares from a haberdasher's, but do consider contrast and visibility for your child. Sew sides together and leave enough space for a funnel to add the filling – rice works very well, or you could add little bells (like those you find on chocolate bunnies or reindeer) to add an audible dimension.

Handout 10
Row, Row, Row Your Boat

Gentle, repetitive vestibular* input is calming and soothing and aids development and integration of the sensory and nervous systems.
If you are not sure of the tune, or just want some help, try these links:

https://youtu.be/R2e2E2b14D0 (Little Baby Bum)

https://youtu.be/EIBd-QoEBQ0 (Dave and Ava Nursery Rhymes)

'Row, Row, Row Your Boat' offers gentle rocking back and forth. It can be soothing or entertaining, depending on what adjustments you make. It develops core strength and specifically targets the vestibular system. The rhyme also helps to develop understanding of forwards and backwards, and push and pull. All you need is a safe place to play!

Sit opposite your child and hold their hands, or put your baby on your lap facing you. Then 'row' back and forwards in time with the music. Start with just the first verse, adding the other verses over time.

Bigger children can sit facing each other cross-legged. Tell them to reach out and hold hands in front of their bodies and begin to alternate pushing and pulling. Their upper bodies rock forward and backward with each motion, like they're rowing a boat. With an older child, see how far he can lean back and still make it back up to sitting position successfully.

If your child needs more support, cradle their back with your arm, or sit them on your knee or between your legs. Some children feel more secure this way.

CHANGE IT UP!

Sit cross-legged with your (small) child on your lap. Start by rolling backwards onto your back. Then, using your legs and abs (this is a good workout for parents/carers, too!), roll back up to sitting again. (Do try first without your child and make sure you *can* get up!) Repeat this motion, rolling forwards and backwards like a boat on the waves. This activity gives much more movement and has the added benefit of full-body deep pressure input, as the child is cuddled up on your lap.

Have the child try it independently: sitting with knees bent (feet on the floor in front of them), they can roll down onto their backs and then up again. A strategically placed cushion may make it easier.

Go back to the original position and add a side-to-side sway. Change the rowing speed, or get your child to give the instructions.

Stand facing the child holding both hands out in front (stand about a foot apart). Slowly extend your arms, the child keeping his body straight and leaning backward and then pull the child gently back toward you. Repeat this rowing motion. Add description to help your child make more sense of the movement.

ROW, ROW, ROW YOUR BOAT

[*Don't forget to squeak, scream and roar when you mention the mouse, crocodile or lion!*]

Row, row, row your boat,
Gently down the stream,
Merrily, merrily, merrily, merrily,
Life is but a dream.

Row, row, row your boat,
Gently up the creek,
If you see a little mouse,
Don't forget to squeak!

Row, row, row your boat,
Gently down the stream,
If you see a crocodile,
Don't forget to scream!

Row, row, row your boat,
Gently to the shore,
If you see a lion,
Don't forget to roar!

Skills covered: trunk stability, sensory integration (emphasis on vestibular), strength, social skills, proprioception,** motor control and grasp.

*The **vestibular** system includes the parts of the inner ear and brain that help control balance, eye movements and spatial orientation.

Proprioception is the sense of self-movement and body position – the relative position of one's own body parts and strength needed to complete each movement (such as how to pick up an egg, without breaking it).

Handout 11
Sessions 1, 2, 3

Wake and Wiggle!
Movement programme
assessment
for _____

Use this document to complete an assessment of the child to show which areas need addressing. If the child has known physical disabilities or conditions, please consult your GP, physiotherapist, or other specialist practitioner who supports your child, before undertaking any exercise programme.

DEVELOPMENTAL MOVEMENT	YES	NO	COMMENTS
Can the child lie on a mat on their tummy?			
Can they lie on a mat on their back?			
Can they lie on their back and raise their legs?			
Can they roll along the mat?			
Are their arms straight?			
Are their legs straight?			
Can they get into a crawling position?			
Can they crawl?			
Do they place their hands down without slapping them?			
Are they able to crawl slowly?			
Are they able to crawl fast?			
Can the child balance themselves when on their knees (in an upright position)?			
Is the child able to do a 'sit-up' with assistance?			
Is the child able to do a 'sit-up' without assistance?			
Is the child able to get into a sitting position on the floor without assistance?			
From a sitting position on the floor, is the child able to stand up without assistance?			
Can they nod/shake their head?			
Can they do a 'thumbs up'?			

RHYTHM AND TIMING	YES	NO	COMMENTS
Can the child make large figure of eight movements with the arms (crossing the midline)?			
Can the child make a large circle movement with their arm – forwards?			
Can the child make a large circle movement with their arm – backwards?			

RHYTHM AND TIMING	YES	NO	COMMENTS
Can the child march on the spot?			
Can they march on the spot and move arms in an alternate rhythmic motion?			

GENERAL/BODY AWARENESS	YES	NO	COMMENTS
Does the child have knowledge of all body parts (see Handout 13)?			
Can the child touch various parts of body on verbal instruction?			
Do they know left and right? Can the child follow instructions about directions?			

MOVEMENT CONCEPTS	YES	NO	COMMENTS
Does the child know...?			
up			
down			
big			
small			
open			
closed			
long			
short			
fast			
slow			
above			
below			
twist			
bend			

MOVEMENT CONCEPTS	YES	NO	COMMENTS
raise			
lower			
in front of			
behind			

BALANCE	YES	NO	COMMENTS
STATIC BALANCE			
Can they stand on their right leg for 10 seconds?			
Can they stand on their left leg for 10 seconds?			
Are their arms still when doing this?			
Do they use their arms to aid balance?			
Is their trunk still when doing this?			
Are their legs not touching each other?			

DYNAMIC BALANCE	YES	NO	COMMENTS
Can they run along a straight line? (Use auditory clues if necessary.)			
Are their arms swinging alternately?			
Can they change direction?			
Can they change pace (fast–slow–fast, etc.)?			
Can they jump with two feet together into a hoop?			
Can they jump with two feet together across the floor?			
Is their jumping pattern rhythmical?			
Can they land on their feet after jumping?			
Can they clear the ground with both feet when jumping?			
Can they hop into a hoop standing on their left foot?			
Can they hop into a hoop standing on their right foot?			

DYNAMIC BALANCE	YES	NO	COMMENTS
Can they hop across the floor on their left leg?			
Can they hop across the floor on their right leg?			
Do they keep upright on landing after hopping?			
Is there a rhythmical pattern when hopping?			
Can they keep their arms and trunk still?			

ADVANCED	YES	NO	COMMENTS
Can the child make a bridge?			
Can they lay on their tummy, and stretch and raise arms and legs off the floor?			
Can they crouch (with assistance)?			
Can they crouch (without assistance)?			
Can they stand on their left leg for 10 seconds?			
Are their arms still when doing this?			
Do they use their arms to aid balance?			
Is their trunk still when doing this?			
Are their legs not touching each other?			
Is the child able to hold a 'plank' position?			

Handout 11a
Wake and Wiggle!
Session 1: Body parts

GUIDANCE

Sort through the suggested YouTube tracks and create a playlist for yourself. This saves a lot of time and effort later, as weblinks do change. YouTube will then run through your routine (with the occasional advert pause).

Repeat these activities until your child no longer needs reminders or physical support to complete them. Children enjoy repetition.

Start activities with a drink. Most people don't drink enough throughout the day, but a cold drink makes the body feel more alert.

BODY PARTS

Before starting Wake and Wiggle!, check the child understands body parts and basic directional concepts. Revise, if necessary. Choose activities that seem closest to your child's current level of understanding.

There are many, many ideas on the internet, but here are a few suggestions to start you off!

WARM-UP

Always do a warm-up before physical exercise. To maximise enjoyment, rehearse all the activities and movement beforehand.

START WITH

'My Body Parts' song, on Elearnin: https://youtu.be/KjQcnlkkP7Y

'Head Shoulders Knees and Toes – Family Sing Along', Muffin Songs: https://youtu.be/YBJ_-MyV2rU

Get the child to sway from side to side in time to the music. If necessary, stand behind him and, using hand over hand, and help him locate the correct body parts. He may be able to do it, but not as fast as the music. This is why it helps to run through the actions first.

MOVE ON TO

'The Skeleton Dance', part of Kids Halloween Songs from Super Simple Songs: https://youtu.be/e54m6XOpRgU

Start off swaying and touching the limbs, then follow the actions.

CALM IT DOWN AND FINISH

'"Row Your Boat" Song with Lyrics - Nursery Rhyme for Kids': https://youtu.be/lkZySVLw4dI

Sit on the floor together using the seating arrangement outlined in Handout 10: Row, Row, Row Your Boat (page 187–188). Try to convey the idea of pushing and pulling, and forwards and backwards.

Handout 11b
Wake and Wiggle!
Session 2

GUIDANCE

Sort through the suggested YouTube tracks and create a playlist for yourself. This saves a lot of time and effort later, as weblinks do change. YouTube will then run through your routine (with the occasional advert pause).

Repeat these activities until your child no longer needs reminders or physical support to complete them. Children enjoy repetition.

Start activities with a drink. Most people don't drink enough throughout the day, but a cold drink makes the body feel more alert.

WARM-UP

Always do a warm-up before physical exercise. To maximise enjoyment, rehearse all the activities and movement beforehand.

Use activities your child already knows well from Session 1. Try making big circles with your arms and progress to making figures of eight with each arm. Stretch up tall and curl up small.

START WITH

'Wake Up! School Assembly Song and Dance from Songs For EVERY Assembly by Out of the Ark Music': https://youtu.be/1gUbdNbu6ak

Some of the actions in this clip (like thumbs up) present more of a challenge, and for children with severe vision impairment they can be difficult to master. To encourage the 'best' movement you can, break the movements down into sections. You may need to be 'hands-on', standing behind a child. If possible, put children into pairs so they can mirror each other.

Each movement should become natural to the child and flow into the next movement in the sequence. The aim is for the child to learn the song and carry out the action corresponding to the word.

LIST OF MOVEMENTS TO LEARN FOR 'WAKE UP!'

Chorus

Arms in big circle – 'Wake up'

Shake body

Run on the spot

Reach up

Jumping jack

Thumbs up!

Arms in big circle – 'new day'

Verse

Make circles with your foot

Arms at chest height, elbows lifted and twist

Hands on ears and move head side to side

Arms in big circle – 'new day'

Then go back to the **Move on to** and **Calm it down and finish** activities from Session 1.

'The Skeleton Dance', part of Kids Halloween Songs from Super Simple Songs: https://youtu.be/e54m6XOpRgU

Start off swaying and touching the limbs, then follow the actions.

'"Row Your Boat" Song with Lyrics - Nursery Rhyme for Kids': https://youtu.be/lkZySVLw4dI

Sit on the floor together using the seating arrangement outlined in Handout 10: Row, Row, Row Your Boat' (page 187–188). Try to convey the idea of pushing and pulling, and forwards and backwards.

Handout 11c
Wake and Wiggle!
Session 3

GUIDANCE

Sort through the suggested YouTube tracks and create a playlist for yourself. This saves a lot of time and effort later, as weblinks do change. YouTube will then run through your routine (with the occasional advert pause).

Repeat these activities until your child no longer needs reminders or physical support to complete them. Children enjoy repetition.

Start activities with a drink. Most people don't drink enough throughout the day, but a cold drink makes the body feel more alert.

WARM-UP

Always do a warm-up before physical exercise. To maximise enjoyment, rehearse all the activities and movement beforehand.

Use activities your child already knows well from Sessions 1 and 2. Try making big circles with your arms and progress to making figures of eight with each arm. Stretch up tall and curl up small.

START WITH

'Wake Up! School Assembly Song and Dance from Songs For EVERY Assembly by Out of the Ark Music': https://youtu.be/1gUbdNbu6ak

Refer back to Session 2 for the details. You can also use any of the previous Wake and Wiggle! activities.

Select some music that appeals to your child and start him sidestepping in time.

MOVE ON TO

Move on to your choice of activities from those outlined below. They will all strengthen core stability and balance.

➢ Animal walking is great fun and really beneficial. Start off on all fours (quadruped) and move round like a dog. Lift one arm up and see if the child can retain his balance as he moves round like an elephant waving its trunk. With his arm down, he can be a cat. Make sure the cat gets some lovely back stretches in and some clawing moves. Transform from the cat into a rabbit or a frog. Remember to get the back legs working to spring forward.

➢ Make an obstacle course. This could include walking across cushions, balancing along a piece of washing line, or crawling through a cardboard box. Use whatever you have to hand. If you have equipment – like a tunnel or stepping stones – use it.

➢ Progress to making a plank, making a bridge or, from the quadruped pose, balancing on three limbs, then two!

➢ If you have a couple of children (or more), use some of the activities in Handout 10: Row, Row, Row Your Boat (pages 187–188) to push and pull and balance against one another. See how far the child can lean back and still successfully come back up to sitting position.

CALM IT DOWN AND FINISH

Warm down with any of the familiar activities from Sessions 1 and 2 that no longer challenge your child.

Handout 12
Early directional concepts

CONCEPT	DEMONSTRATE WITH PHYSICAL MOVEMENT	TICK OR DATE			
here	Here it is – locate using sound or vision				
	Come here				
up	Pick me up				
down	Get down/lie down				
in	Come in				
out	Go out				
on	Sit on the chair				
off	Get off the chair				
behind	I'm behind you!				
in front	Reach in front				
next to	Sit next to me				
stop	Stop in response to voice instruction				
go	Ready, steady, go!				

These directional concepts can all be developed using gross motor movement in play.

The adult may be in physical contact with the child. Create the movement, describe it and emphasise the main concept. Doing this both creates and reinforces motor memory.

Establishing voice control and a consistent response to 'Stop' is essential before a child can be permitted to free-walk in more dangerous areas.

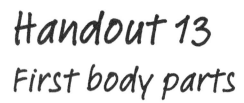

Handout 13
First body parts

Tick or add comments in the table (as appropriate).

Head				
Eyes				
Ears				
Mouth				
Nose				
Hands				
Fingers				
Feet				
Toes				
Tummy				
Bottom				
Arm				
Leg				

ACTIVITIES

➢ Play 'Simon Says'. Try and find ways to touch body parts on the opposite side (for example, left hand touches right ear).

➢ Lie the child on a roll of wallpaper and draw round their body. Once the child has got up again, label all the body parts together.

➢ Make pictures using handprints and footprints.

Handout 14
Stop, look and listen
Road safety information for parents of children with visual impairments

PLEASE DO ✓

✓ Use the phrase 'Stop, look and listen' when you are crossing roads together.

✓ Try walking to a local pelican or puffin crossing, and get your child to show you how it should work. Let him press the button and tell you when it is safe to cross.

✓ Try crossing a zebra crossing together. Show him a belisha beacon.

✓ Talk about waiting for traffic to stop and making safe decisions to cross.

✓ Hold hands with very young children. If you want to introduce a degree of freedom, try using reins. Only let your child free-walk when you are sure you have voice control and he responds immediately to 'Stop'.

✓ Explain safer crossing places, and why he should use them.

PLEASE DON'T ✗

✗ Cross against the lights (children do pick up bad habits).

✗ Avoid using a controlled crossing if there is one available.

✗ Cross between parked cars.

✗ Hold an older child's hand crossing the road. Let her take your arm if she wishes, but encourage her to take more responsibility for her own safety while you are still there to supervise.

Handout 15
I'm lost!

You are not lost – you're just separated from the people who care for you. They are looking for you, so this is what you should do:

Stop. Stand still, look and listen carefully.

Can you see or hear the person you are with?
Yes? Are you sure?
If you are absolutely sure, go straight to them and hold their hand.

No? Stand still and listen.
Are they calling your name?
Yes? Can you see or hear them? If not, wait for them to come
    to you.

If you still can't see or hear them, can you see or hear the tills in
    the shop?
Only go to the tills or checkout in a shop if you are sure you can
    find them.

Never leave a shop with anybody other than the person you went
    in with.

If you are in the street or a shopping centre, wait a while. Then go
    into the biggest shop you can find and seek help at the tills.

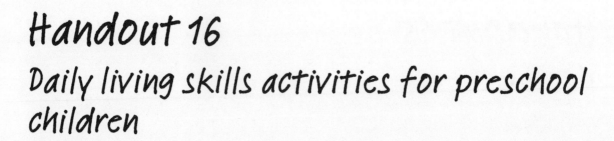

Handout 16
Daily living skills activities for preschool children

These activities are really skills for life. Therefore, start them as early as possible and involve everyone who works with the child. Use the same approach and language with the child, so that (for example) directional instruction remains the same. This avoids confusion for both the child and the adults!

TOILETING

✓ Bribery (in any form) rules! Keep a packet of Smarties or similar on hand. Or use taped songs or favourite toys – anything that constitutes a reward.

✓ Use the same routine every time when entering and leaving the toilet. Think about a simple route in and out, and add any tactile points in the room that the child may understand (bells on the door, elastic band on the handle, for example).

✓ Be flexible about the use of the potty or toilet. A lot of visually impaired children fear sitting on a toilet. Do not leave the child on their own. Do offer lots of talk and support, such as holding hands. Singing aloud helps, too!

✓ Some children need to 'look' at what they have done and where it is! Don't be too squeamish about it. However, it can be discouraged once the child develops the skill.

✓ Use the flush system as a reward. Most children love to hear it and do it for themselves.

✓ Be sure the child always does the whole process, including handwashing, every time.

✓ Make a huge fuss at every success. Accept accidents – and there will be many! Take the child to the bathroom to change their wet clothes, so that the act becomes associated with the appropriate places.

EATING

✓ Fingers were invented before forks, so concentrate on them first.

✓ Many visually impaired children develop preferences for hard-edged foods, like burgers and chips. They dislike foods with poor definition, such as yoghurt with bits in. Give a commentary about what you are offering them to eat.

✓ A Dycem® mat (or damp cloth) under a child's plate keeps the plate still and facing in the same direction.

✓ Try to used rimmed plates with a good colour contrast with the table – for example, blue on yellow.

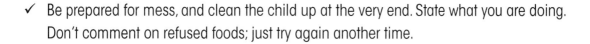

✓ Use the hand on hand technique when starting to use tools. Begin with a spoon and fork. Some cutlery has enlarged grips and this may prove useful.

✓ Be prepared for mess, and clean the child up at the very end. State what you are doing. Don't comment on refused foods; just try again another time.

✓ Let the child feel your own jaw when you're chewing and listen to you eating crunchy foods. They will love it!

DRESSING AND UNDRESSING

✓ Encourage easy clothes like tracksuit bottoms. All fastenings are a problem and make everyone frustrated. Avoid getting heads stuck!

✓ Begin by letting the child do as much or little as they can, which may be pulling off a sock. Praise, praise, praise!

✓ Arrange clothing on a chair, where the child can return to dress again. Place items over the chair back – in the order that they come off. Put socks and shoes underneath the chair.

✓ The backs of clothing can be marked with a small button, or a piece of Velcro® on the neck label. Choose Velcro® wherever you can, as children love the sound of it. They love zips, too!

Appendices

✓ Place coats with hoods on the back of the child's head, as a start to putting the coat on. Add extra length to zips – use a safety pin or paper clip to ease movement up and down.

✓ Provide a variety of fastenings on good-quality cloth for the child to play with.

✓ Be patient and praise every time. Occasionally, try to put the child in a position where there is no time pressure for dressing and undressing.

Appendix 4: Songs, rhymes and story bags

This appendix contains two sets of activities.

Activity 1 presents a selection of songs and rhymes to develop body awareness, gross and fine motor skills, finger isolation and hand strength, balance and core stability and spatial awareness. These also develop key concepts, vocabulary and language and social skills.

Activity 2 explains how you can create story bags to use when working with your child. It lists examples of a variety of useful stories, along with the concepts and topics they cover.

Activity 1
Songs and rhymes

CONCEPTS AND TOPICS

Singing is so good for you – and it's good for your child, too. It encourages you to bond with your child. It makes you both feel happy and boosts your immune systems, and helps to teach children and babies about language. What's more, singing develops the lips and tongue, and develops memory skills. Combine singing with actions, and your child's coordination and motor skills will also improve.

The rhymes listed below will promote body awareness, balance and movement skills, and help with naming different parts of the body and developing concepts. This is just a starting point, though. You can find more information and ideas in the links listed below.

Buy yourself a good nursery action rhyme book. My favourite is *Round and Round the Garden* (see below), but other more up-to-date publications are available. These include:

Felicity Brooks (ed.) (2011) *Usborne Illustrated Nursery Rhymes*. London: Usborne Publishing.

Axel Scheffler (2009) *Mother Goose's Action Rhymes*. London: Macmillan.

Sarah Williams (2006) *Round and Round the Garden*. Oxford: Oxford University Press.

DEM BONES

➢ Body awareness

➢ Body parts and how they connect

DINGLY DANGLY SCARECROW

➢ Body awareness

➢ Balance

GRAND OLD DUKE OF YORK

➢ Up and down

➢ Marching skills

HEADS, SHOULDERS, KNEES AND TOES

➢ Body parts

➢ Body awareness

➢ Spatial awareness

HICKORY DICKORY DOCK

➢ Rhythm of this rhyme is ideal for tapping a long cane while walking

HOKEY COKEY

➢ Body parts

➢ Right and left

➢ Balance and coordination

IF YOU'RE HAPPY AND YOU KNOW IT

➢ General movement

➢ Spatial awareness

➢ Bilateral movement

ONE FINGER, ONE THUMB

➢ Finger isolation

➢ Awareness of hands

➢ Manual dexterity

RIDE A COCK HORSE

➢ Core stability

➢ Balance

➢ Rhythm

ROUND AND ROUND THE GARDEN

➢ Aids awareness of hands, your hands, my hands

➢ Anticipation

ROW, ROW, ROW YOUR BOAT

➢ Concepts of forwards/backwards

➢ Strength for/understanding of pull and push

THIS LITTLE PIGGY

➢ Awareness of toes and toe separation

➢ Anticipation

TOMMY THUMB

Words and music anonymous

➢ Finger separation

➢ Individual finger identification, size and length

WIND THE BOBBIN UP

➢ Orientation within a room

➢ Up, down

➢ Pointing, winding, pulling, clapping

➢ Bilateral hand movement

THE WHEELS ON THE BUS

➢ Travel

➢ Round

➢ Movement

➢ Up/down

➢ Side to side

ROW, ROW, ROW YOUR BOAT

Row, row, row your boat,
Gently down the stream,
Merrily, merrily, merrily, merrily,
Life is but a dream.

Alternate the last two lines with 'If you see a crocodile, don't forget to scream!'

IF YOU'RE HAPPY AND YOU KNOW IT

If you're happy and you know it, clap your hands [clap clap].
If you're happy and you know it, clap your hands [clap clap].
If you're happy and you know it, then you surely want to show it.
If you're happy and you know it, clap your hand.

Other verses:
…, snap your fingers [snap snap].
…, touch your head [touch touch].

You can touch any other body part, too. Do the actions stated in the song – clap your hands, stomp your feet, etc. Get the children to do the motions with you.

TOMMY THUMB

Tommy Thumb, Tommy Thumb, where are you?
Here I am, here I am. How do you do?

Peter Pointer, Peter Pointer, where are you?
Here I am, here I am. How do you do?
Finger Tall, Finger Tall, where are you?
Here I am, here I am. How do you do?

Ruby Ring, Ruby Ring, where are you?
Here I am, here I am. How do you do?

Baby Small, Baby Small, where are you?
Here I am, here I am. How do you do?

Fingers All, where are you?
Here I am, here I am. How do you do?

THE GRAND OLD DUKE OF YORK

Oh, the grand old Duke of York,
He had ten thousand men,
He marched them up to the top of the hill,
And he marched them down again.
And when they were up, they were up,
And when they were down, they were down,
And when they were only halfway up,
They were neither up nor down.
[repeat]

WIND THE BOBBIN UP

Wind the bobbin up,
Wind the bobbin up,
Pull, pull, clap, clap, clap.

Wind it back again,
Wind it back again,
Pull, pull, clap, clap, clap.

Point to the ceiling,
Point to the floor,
Point to the window,
Point to the door,
Put your hands together one, two, three.

Now put your hands upon your knee,
Wind the bobbin up,
Wind the bobbin up,
Pull, pull, clap, clap, clap.

This 'Wind the Bobbin Up' YouTube link follows onto lots more rhymes: https://youtu.be/
7IxQb1oHCHM

DRY BONES (OR SKELETON BONES OR DEM BONES, DEM DRY BONES)

Oh those bones, oh those bones,
oh those skeleton bones.
Oh those bones, oh those bones,
oh those skeleton bones.
Oh those bones, oh those bones,
oh those skeleton bones.
Oh mercy how they scare!

With the toe bone connected
to the foot bone,
and the foot bone connected
to the ankle bone,
and the ankle bone connected
to the leg bone.
Oh mercy how they scare!

Oh those bones, oh those bones,
oh those skeleton bones.
Oh those bones, oh those bones,
oh those skeleton bones.
Oh those bones, oh those bones,
oh those skeleton bones.
Oh mercy how they scare!

With the leg bone connected
to the knee bone,
and the knee bone connected
to the thigh bone,
and the thigh bone connected
to the hip bone.
Oh mercy how they scare!

Oh those bones, oh those bones,
oh those skeleton bones.
Oh those bones, oh those bones,
oh those skeleton bones.
Oh those bones, oh those bones,
oh those skeleton bones.
Oh mercy how they scare!

With the hip bone connected
to the back bone,
and the back bone connected
to the neck bone,
and the neck bone connected
to the head bone,
Oh mercy how they scare!

Oh those bones, oh those bones,
oh those skeleton bones.
Oh those bones, oh those bones,
oh those skeleton bones.
Oh those bones, oh those bones,
oh those skeleton bones.
Oh mercy how they scare!

With the finger bone connected
to the hand bone,
and the hand bone connected
to the arm bone,
and the arm bone connected
to the shoulder bone,
Oh mercy how they scare!

Oh those bones, oh those bones,
oh those skeleton bones.
Oh those bones, oh those bones,
oh those skeleton bones.
Oh those bones, oh those bones,
oh those skeleton bones.
Oh mercy how they scare!

With the shoulder bone connected
to the back bone,
and the back bone connected
to the neck bone,
and the neck bone connected
to the head bone.
Oh mercy how they scare!

HOKEY COKEY

You put your left arm in, your left arm out,
In out, in out, you shake it all about,
You do the Hokey Cokey and you turn around,
That's what it's all about.
Whoa-o the Hokey Cokey,
Whoa-o the Hokey Cokey,
Whoa-o the Hokey Cokey,
Knees bent, arms stretched,
Raa raa raa.

You put your right arm in, your right arm out,
In out, in out, you shake it all about,
You do the Hokey Cokey and you turn around,
That's what it's all about.
Whoa-o the Hokey Cokey,
Whoa-o the Hokey Cokey,
Whoa-o the Hokey Cokey,
Knees bent, arms stretched,
Raa raa raa.

You put your left leg in, your left leg out,
In out, in out, you shake it all about,
You do the Hokey Cokey and you turn around,
That's what it's all about.
Whoa-o the Hokey Cokey,
Whoa-o the Hokey Cokey,
Whoa-o the Hokey Cokey,
Knees bent, arms stretched,
Raa raa raa.

You put your right leg in, your right leg out,
In out, in out, you shake it all about,
You do the Hokey Cokey and you turn around,
That's what it's all about.
Whoa-o the Hokey Cokey,
Whoa-o the Hokey Cokey,
Whoa-o the Hokey Cokey,
Knees bent, arms stretched,
Raa raa raa.

You put your whole self in, your whole self out,
In out, in out, you shake it all about,
You do the Hokey Cokey and you turn around,
That's what it's all about.
Whoa-o the Hokey Cokey,
Whoa-o the Hokey Cokey,
Whoa-o the Hokey Cokey,
Knees bent, arms stretched,
Raa raa raa.

Whoa-o the Hokey Cokey,
Whoa-o the Hokey Cokey,
Whoa-o the Hokey Cokey,
Knees bent, arms stretched,
Raa raa raa.

DINGLY DANGLY SCARECROW

When all the cows are sleeping,
And the farmer's gone to bed,
Up jumps the scarecrow,
And this is what he says!

I'm a dingly dangly scarecrow,
With a flippy floppy hat,
I can shake my hands like this,
I can shake my feet like that.

HICKORY DICKORY DOCK

Tick tock, tick tock,
Hickory dickory dock,
The mouse ran up the clock,
The clock struck one,
The mouse was gone,
Hickory dickory dock.

HEADS, SHOULDERS, KNEES AND TOES

Heads, shoulders, knees and toes, knees and toes.
Heads, shoulders, knees and toes, knees and toes.
And eyes and ears and mouth and nose…
Heads, shoulders, knees and toes, knees and toes.

ROUND AND ROUND THE GARDEN

Round and round the garden,
Like a teddy bear,
One step, two step,
And tickly under there.

THIS LITTLE PIGGY

This little piggy went to market,
This little piggy stayed at home,
This little piggy had roast beef,
And this little piggy had none,
And this little piggy went wee, wee, wee, all the way home!

RIDE A COCK HORSE

Ride a cock horse to Banbury Cross,
To see a fine lady upon a white horse,
With rings on her fingers and bells on her toes,
She shall have music wherever she goes.

ONE FINGER, ONE THUMB

One finger, one thumb, keep moving,
One finger, one thumb, keep moving,
One finger, one thumb, keep moving,
We'll all be merry and bright.

One finger, one thumb, one arm, keep moving [3 times],
We'll all be merry and bright.

One finger, one thumb, one arm, one leg, keep moving [3 times],
We'll all be merry and bright.

One finger, one thumb, one arm, one leg, one nod of the head, keep moving [3 times],
We'll all be merry and bright.

One finger, one thumb, one arm, one leg, one nod of the head, stand up, keep moving
[3 times]
We'll all be merry and bright.

One finger, one thumb, one arm, one leg, one nod of the head, stand up, sit down, keep moving [3 times],
We'll all be merry and bright.

THE WHEELS ON THE BUS

The wheels on the bus go round and round,
Round and round, Round and round,

The wheels on the bus go round and round,
All day long.

The wipers on the bus go swish, swish, swish,
Swish, swish, swish,
Swish, swish, swish,

The wipers on the bus go swish, swish, swish,
All day long

The horn on the bus goes beep, beep, beep,
Beep, beep, beep,
Beep, beep, beep

The horn on the bus goes beep, beep, beep,
all day long.

Add your own verses, too:

The mummies on the bus go chatter, chatter, chatter,...
The children on the bus jump up and down,...
The babies on the bus go 'waaah, waaah, waaah',...

ONLINE RESOURCES

YouTube has loads of helpful rhymes and songs. Many will remind you of the actions if you are not sure, search on You Tube or Spotify for 'Little Baby Bum', which has lovely clear images and demonstrates the actions clearly.

Activity 2
Create your own story bags

There are some wonderful story bags listed in educational catalogues. As well as often being very expensive, they don't necessarily provide the input a child with a vision impairment needs in order to develop a concept.

1. Decide which concepts or topics you want to address.

2. Look for a mainstream children's book that incorporates your concept or topic. Old, tried and tested favourites are usually popular for a good reason. To keep the cost down, ask around if someone has an unwanted copy of the book. Failing that, buy second-hand copies of the book. Look on amazon. co.uk or sites like www.worldofbooks.com/en-gb, alibris. co.uk and abebooks.co.uk.

3. Pick up cheap canvas bags (whenever you see them) to store the book and props. Photocopy the front cover of the book – this will be the story bag's label. Put a list of the bag's contents on the back of the label, then laminate it.

4. If you or a colleague have any craft skills, you could make props to go in the bag. Alternatively, consider visiting charity shops to get your main characters, or ask friends and family if they have anything suitable.

5. Start with the story examples listed below. You'll be moving onto your own projects in no time, however.

LITTLE RED RIDING HOOD

You will need

➢ Copy of *Little Red Riding Hood*. This ladybird touch and feel book is ideal.

➢ **Wolf and Grandma toys.** This Ikea one is ideal, but only available second hand now. Use puppets or transforming dolls instead.

➢ **Little Red Riding Hood** – doll or puppet. Make a cloak if necessary.

➢ Suitable **worksheets** and activities from Twinkl, or create your own.

➢ **Canvas bag** to hold the contents.

Total actual cost: less than £10.

Concepts and topics

➢ Personal safety.

➢ Stranger awareness.

➢ Following instructions.

➢ Caring for others.

➢ What to do if things go wrong.

GOLDILOCKS AND THE THREE BEARS

You will need

➤ A copy of **Goldilocks and the Three Bears.** Any will do, but the Ladybird Touch and Feel book is ideal.

➤ A **doll**, ideally with long blonde hair and sized appropriate to the bears.

➤ **Three teddy bears** of different sizes, with appropriate accessories (these could be handmade).

➤ **Worksheets** and activities downloaded from Twinkl, or add and create your own.

➤ A box for storage and to act as the Three Bears' house. A discarded Build-a-Bear® **box** is ideal.

Concepts and topics

➤ Personal safety.

➤ Stranger awareness.

➤ Respect for others and their property.

➤ Sizes – big, medium and small.

➤ Hard and soft.

➤ Hot and cold.

➤ What to do if things go wrong.

Expand this topic by making porridge together.

MY CAT LIKES TO HIDE IN BOXES

(Eve Sutton, Puffin)

You will need

➢ Copies (more than one is good – just in case!) of **My Cat Likes to Hide in Boxes**.

➢ **Cardboard boxes** – various sizes.

➢ **Cat toy** (this needs to be small enough to fit into the boxes)

➢ **Canvas bag** to hold the contents.

Concepts and topics

➢ Big and little.

➢ In and out.

➢ Open and closed.

➢ Up and down.

➢ Different countries.

➢ Different actions and movements.

OTHER STORIES – CONCEPTS AND TOPICS

The Three Little Pigs

➢ Construction materials.

➢ Personal safety.

Is That You, Wolf?
(Steve Cox)

➢ Personal safety.

➢ Mild anxiety.

➢ Tactile skills.

Postman Pat
(John Cunliffe)

➢ Postal system.

➢ Helping and caring for others.

The Great Pet Sale
(Mick Inkpen)

➢ Animals, pets and wild animals.

➢ Handling money.

Glossary

WHO/WHAT/WHERE	DESCRIPTION
Action on Hearing Loss	Action on Hearing Loss, formerly RNID (Royal National Insitute for the Deaf) provides support for people with hearing loss, deafness and tinnitus. www.actiononhearingloss.org.uk/
Attachment	'Attachment' is the term for the emotional bond an infant forms with the primary caregiver, usually the mother. The term 'bonding' is used to describe the emotions of love and responsibility that parents develop for the child.
Attachment disorder	The failure to develop a successful secure bond between child and caregiver. It covers a range of emotional and behavioural problems.
Attention difficulties/ ADHD	Attention deficit hyperactivity disorder (*ADHD*) is a behavioural disorder that includes symptoms such as inattentiveness, hyperactivity and impulsiveness. Symptoms of *ADHD* tend to be noticed at an early age and may become more noticeable when a child's circumstances change, such as when they start school.
Autistic Spectrum Condition (ASC)	Also referred to as ASD/Autistic Spectrum Disorder. Some children with severe sight impairment show traits of ASC, but do not have a diagnosis, because it stems from lack of knowledge of the world and improves over time. Some children may have sight impairment and an ASC diagnosis.
Backward chaining	See **Chaining**.
BATOD (British Association of Teachers of the Deaf)	BATOD is the only association in the United Kingdom that represents the interests of teachers of deaf children and young people: www.batod.org.uk/information/training-as-a-teacher-of-the-deaf/
Braille	Braille is a tactile reading and writing system, created by Louis Braille in the nineteenth century and still in use today. It can be produced on a Perkins Brailler (see below) or on an electronic device like a BrailleNote. It works by producing a series of raised dots using variations of a six-dot cell.
British Blind Sport (BBS)	Go to https://britishblindsport.org.uk/ for information on early movement programmes, including First Steps and Jangles.

WHO/WHAT/WHERE	DESCRIPTION
CAMHS (Child and Adolescent Mental Health Service)	CAMHS is likely to be involved if your child has an ASC (Autism Spectrum Condition) diagnosis or has other acute mental health issues.
Cerebra	Cerebra is the national charity helping children with brain conditions and their families discover a better life together. They give lots of good advice on their website, and are particularly good on sleep issues. They offer a specialist one-to-one advice and support service for children with certain diagnoses (https://cerebra.org.uk/get-advice-support/sleep-advice-service/, https://cerebra.org.uk/).
Chaining	When teaching any complex task, it is necessary to break it into small component parts. These tasks are taught separately, but are sequential. Teaching them step by step is known as chaining. Success is key to progress, so you start with the element the child is most likely to achieve. Forward chaining starts with the beginning of the task sequence. After each step is mastered, instruction begins at the next step. The remainder of the task is completed each time by the adult modelling and explaining actions. Backward chaining starts with learning the final component and working backwards through the components. Jerry Webster, 'Chaining Forward and Chaining Backwards.' *ThoughtCo*, 30 January 2019. www.thoughtco.com/chaining-forward-and-chaining-backwards-3110581
Changing Places	To use the toilet in safety and comfort, many people need to be able to access Changing Places, which have more space and the right equipment, including a height-adjustable changing bench and a hoist. You can find more information and locations on www.changing-places.org/
Child Development Centre (CDC)	The CDC is a centre that offers multi-disciplinary assessment for children from birth until they start school at 4 years of age. The team sees preschool children who may have a delay in their development or some other special need. Some difficulties are identified at birth; others become apparent or develop as a child grows. This delay may include additional needs in a number of areas, such as vision, hearing, speech, physical and emotional development, and/or learning difficulties. Problems can be temporary and disappear as the child gets older, or they may be more permanent.
Child protection	See **Safeguarding**.

WHO/WHAT/WHERE	DESCRIPTION
ClearVision Project	ClearVision is a postal lending library of children's books designed to be shared by visually impaired and sighted children and adults. They will loan books all across the UK and Ireland. All books have Braille, print and pictures. This allows children with little or no sight to share books with their sighted friends and family, and adult Braille readers to enjoy stories with sighted children. There are over 14,000 books in the collection, catering for children from birth until they're independent readers.
Code of Practice (SEND)	This Code of Practice provides statutory guidance on duties, policies and procedures relating to Part 3 of the Children and Families Act 2014 and associated regulations and applies to England. It relates to children and young people with special educational needs (SEN) and disabled children and young people. It provides the framework for EHCPs (see entry below). Department for Education/Department of Health (2015) *Special Educational Needs and Disability Code of Practice: 0 to 25 Years*, January. London: DfE/DoH. https://assets.publishing.service.gov.uk/government/uploads/system/uploads/attachment_data/file/398815/SEND_Code_of_Practice_January_2015.pdf
Demonstration	You can demonstrate skills practically in a variety of ways, either visually, where the child can see enough to copy what you are doing or tactilely, by using hand over hand or hand under hand so the child can feel what you are doing.
Developmental journals	The *Developmental Journal for Babies and Young Children with Vision Impairment (DJVI)* was created by Alison Dale and Naomi Salt to be used, in partnership with parents, by qualified clinicians and specialist professionals working in services providing support to babies and young children with visual impairment and their parents. A licence currently costs £100 (https://xip.uclb.com/i/healthcare_tools/DJVI_professional.html). The original free version can still be found here (at the time of publication): www.childreninwales.org.uk/wp-content/uploads/2015/09/Developmental-Journal-Visual-impairment.pdf and here: www.narhu.org/wp-content/uploads/2016/02/1.1.-perceptual-development-visual_impairment_information_for_parents.pdf and you can find the activity cards here: http://priestleysmith.co.uk/wp-content/uploads/2019/11/developmental_journal_for_babies_and_children_with_visual_impairment_-_activity_cards.pdf
Dexterity	Manual dexterity is the ability to make small, precise, coordinated hand and finger movements to grasp and manipulate objects. Development of these skills occurs over time, primarily during childhood. It requires motor planning and complex execution of a task.

WHO/WHAT/WHERE	DESCRIPTION
Dog, Duck and Cat Trust	Dog, Duck and Cat Trust provide a range of stories and activities for parents, carers and professionals covering a wide range of social and safety issues. All content is matched to the new RSE curriculum. https://www.dogduckandcat.co.uk/
Dysphagia	Dysphagia is the medical term for swallowing difficulties. Some people with dysphagia have problems swallowing certain foods or liquids, while others can't swallow at all. Other signs of dysphagia include: ✓ coughing or choking when eating or drinking ✓ bringing food back up, sometimes through the nose ✓ a sensation that food is stuck in your throat or chest ✓ persistent drooling of saliva ✓ being unable to chew food properly ✓ a 'gurgly' wet-sounding voice when eating or drinking.
Education Health and Care Plan (EHCP)	The Education Health Care Plan replaced the Statement of Special Educational Needs. It is a legal document that describes a child or young person's special educational, health and social care needs and shows how those needs will be met. They can apply to children and young people between the ages of 0 and 25.
Emotional literacy	*Emotional literacy* is the term used to describe the ability to understand and express feelings. It requires children to recognise their own feelings and manage them, and is a skill that all children need to develop. There are five main aspects of emotional intelligence which, when developed, lead to children becoming emotionally literate. In his book *Emotional Intelligence*, Daniel Goleman identifies: ✓ Knowing emotions – a child recognises a feeling as it happens ✓ Managing emotions – a child has ways of reassuring themselves when they feel anxious or upset ✓ Self-motivation – a child is in charge of their emotions, rather than controlled by them ✓ Empathy – a child is aware of what another person is feeling ✓ Handling relationships – child is able to build relationships with others. See also: www.elsa-support.co.uk/ www.parentkind.org.uk/blog/8719/ Helping-children-develop-emotional-literacy
Grief	You, your family members or your child may grieve for their sight loss. This may seem strange, but the grief stems from the loss of the life you were expecting. You may wish to seek specialist counselling.

WHO/WHAT/WHERE	DESCRIPTION
Guide Dogs: Children and Young People's Services	Children and Young People's Services are now an integral part of Guide Dogs. They provide habilitation and other support to children and young people with vision impairments, either independently or through local authority contracts. Guide dogs and buddy dogs are available to qualifying children and young people. www.guidedogs.org.uk/services-we-provide
Habilitation assistant	An habilitation assistant provides work to children and families under the direction of the habilitation specialist.
Habilitation specialist	An habilitation specialist holds a professional qualification and should be registered as a Qualified Habilitation Specialist, RQHS with HabilitationVIUK. They teach orientation and mobility skills and independent living skills at home and at school, depending on where you child is educated. This can include teaching a child how to use a cane, teaching specific routes around school or the local area, road safety, personal safety and the range of life skills in this book.
HabilitationVIUK	This is the professional body for UK habilitation specialists and assistants. There are webpages for parents and professionals. www.habilitationviuk.org.uk
Hand over hand	When you use the hand over hand technique to help your child do an activity, you place your hands over your child's hands. Wherever possible, work from behind your child. Your child is the one who is touching the materials, and your hands guide them as they manipulate the materials to complete the activity. As you find they are able to do small parts of the activity, you can lessen the support your hands provide by pulling your hands away or moving them to their wrist or arm. In that way, your hands are ready to come back and lend support if your child needs assistance.
Hand under hand	When you use the hand under hand technique, your hands perform the activity while your child's hands rest on top of yours— this way, your child can feel what your hands are doing. If the activity is new to your child and they are hesitant to try it, they may feel more secure touching your hands rather than the unknown object or activity. Also, because their palms are on your hands, they'll be able to focus their energy on feeling the movements of your hands. They may also feel more comfortable and in control because they can freely remove their hands if they want to. As you perform the activity, describe what you are doing with your hands. Always try to work from behind your child, or alongside, if possible.

WHO/WHAT/WHERE	DESCRIPTION
Health visitor	Heath visitors provide health care and development support to children and families from birth until the child starts school. There are generic health visitors as well as some who take on special interests. Your GP can put you in touch if you are not already in contact.
Incidental learning	Incidental Learning is what a child absorbs from watching and mimicking parents, siblings or peers. The vast majority of learning usually comes through vision, but this information stream is lost to children with severe vision impairment. These children need to be specifically taught many elements that other children just assimilate. It can mean that babies and children develop at a slower rate and have less understanding of the world around them, without early targeted intervention.
IPSEA (Independent Provider of Special Education Advice)	*IPSEA* offers independent legally based advice, support and training to help get the right education for children and young people with special educational needs. They offer a unique range of services developed to make sure that families, and those advising them, understand children and young people's legal rights and entitlements to education provision. www.ipsea.org.uk/
Little Room (Dr Lilli Nielsen)	The Little Room is one element of Active Learning (AL), which is designed for learners with significant disabilities. It provides great stimulation for babies and children with severe sight impairment. Originated by Dr Lilli Nielsen, the Danish expert, AL is suitable for learners who have a developmental age of 4 or under. Little Rooms: https://lilliworks.org/al-items/major-items/ A Little Room in action: https://youtu.be/X7_S4dfN_-U
Look UK	Look is on a mission to support young visually impaired people and their families to thrive. They do this through mentoring, transformational events, youth forums and parent support groups. www.look-uk.org/
National Quality Standards for Habilitation Training	These Quality Standards are designed to make sure that children and young people with visual impairment are enabled (through high-quality mobility and independence training and support) to achieve the greatest possible independence and maximise their educational outcomes and life chances. The Standards are currently under review, but can be found here until they're revised: https://habilitationviuk.org.uk/welcome-habilitation-vi-uk__trashed/national-quality-standards-habilitation-training/ www.ssc.education.ed.ac.uk/resources/vi&multi/habilitation.pdf

WHO/WHAT/WHERE	DESCRIPTION
Object permanence	Object permanence is the understanding that objects continue to exist even when they cannot be perceived (seen, heard, touched, smelled or sensed in any way). The term was coined by **Jean Piaget** (see below) and is considered to be one of the earliest ways of evaluating 'working memory'. https://youtu.be/E-I98QArglo
Objects of reference	These are tactile objects that reinforce understanding of activities, things or locations. Your child may have a tactile timetable in school. Some suggestions for objects of reference: ✓ swimsuit for swimming ✓ pumps/trainers for PE ✓ toilet roll for toilet ✓ flannel for bath or washing. Try and avoid transient objects of reference that may build in limits or cause confusion. For instance, don't use a nappy for the toilet and don't use armbands for swimming (because they become redundant: a child gets potty-trained and learns to swim).
Occupational therapist (OT)	Occupational therapists treat injured, ill or disabled patients through the therapeutic use of everyday activities. They help these patients develop, recover, improve (as well as maintain) the skills needed for daily living and working.
Paediatrician	A consultant doctor who specialises in the care of children and young people
Perkins Brailler	The Perkins School for the Blind is the home of the Perkins Brailler. It is primarily a day and residential school (in Massachusetts) for children and young people with vision impairment. They also offer helpful blogs, a wide range of resources and links to other useful sites, as well as their educational hub (which includes Paths to Literacy, which holds a phenomenal range of resources and ideas). www.perkins.org/
Physiotherapist	A physiotherapist helps restore movement and function when someone is affected by injury, illness or disability. You can access physiotherapy through your GP, by self-referral or via a specialist (depending on how your local NHS systems are set up). Some special schools have specialist physiotherapists based on site. You can also obtain physiotherapy privately.

WHO/WHAT/WHERE	DESCRIPTION
Piaget, Jean	Jean Piaget was a Swiss psychologist known for his work on child development. His theory contained four distinct stages of cognitive development in children: sensorimotor, preoperational, concrete and formal. He placed great emphasis on the education of children. He first coined the term 'object permanence', which develops during the sensorimotor stage (see above). Find out more at https://youtu.be/IhcgYgx7aAA or in Meggitt (2012), in the chapter on child development theories.
Proprioception	Proprioception uses the feedback from muscles and joints and works in conjunction with the vestibular system to enable the brain to calculate the body's position in relation to balance, direction, movement and force. In simple terms: ✓ it allows the brain to work out how much force it needs to grasp and pick up a raw eggshell without breaking it ✓ it enables the calculations that adjust leg extension and stride to run up a hill without falling.
Protective behaviours	Protective Behaviours is a safety awareness and resilience-building programme. It helps children and adults to recognise any situation where they feel worried or unsafe, such as feeling stressed, bullied or threatened, and explores practical ways to keep safe. Children are taught that they can talk about anything, no matter how big or small, to their chosen safe people. It encourages the use of correct medical terminology from an early age for genitals and other body parts, to avoid confusion. www.protectivebehaviours.org/what-does-protective-behaviours-mean
QTVI (Qualified Teacher of Vision impaired) or **TOVI (teacher of vision impaired)**	QTVI is a mandatory qualification for those exclusively teaching children and young people with vision impairments. All children with SVI should have access to a QTVI from time to time. Find out more about the role from the RNIB: www.rnib.org.uk/services-we-offer-advice-professionals/education-professionals
Radar Key	Many disabled toilets are locked with a Radar Key to ensure they are available for disabled people when necessary, and to prevent damage. There is more room and they are quite often cleaner than other public toilets. These keys are universal – you may be able to obtain one through Social Care, from Disability Rights UK or on Amazon. If you child is bigger or needs more support, look into Changing Places (see above).
Reflexes	The primitive reflexes in a one month old can be seen here: https://youtu.be/vdiCep6OStA

WHO/WHAT/WHERE	DESCRIPTION
Resonance board	The sounds that a child produces on a resonance board will be transmitted through the wood and will be felt by the child on other parts of his/her body. The sounds will be supplemented by a tactile effect, which is important to the child's motivation for increased activity. http://activelearningspace.org/equipment/purchase-equipment/the-resonance-board
Resource base (VI base within a school)	A number of mainstream schools contain resource bases within them. The student attends a mainstream school, but is afforded additional support through the resource base. In the case of VI bases, there should be a QTVI (see above) on site and support varies depending on need, but can include facilitating a student to access what is on the board or teaching Braille or touch typing.
RNIB (Royal National Institute of Blind People)	The RNIB offers a variety of support services and leaflets and campaigns on behalf of those with vision impairment. The RNIB has pages for people with sight loss, and their families and professionals: www.rnib.org.uk/
Safeguarding	All schools or other organisations working with children must undertake regular safeguarding training and be cognisant of the relevant statutory guidance. In schools it is the *Keeping Children Safe in Education* document, which is revised annually: www.gov.uk/government/publications/keeping-children-safe-in-education--2 Staff should all hold enhanced DBS (Disclosure and Barring Service) status. A full list of Government current safeguarding documents can be found at: www.gov.uk/topic/schools-colleges-childrens-services/safeguarding-children
Safety	For advice on keeping your child safe: ✓ Child Accident Prevention Trust: www.capt.org.uk/ ✓ Dog, Duck & Cat Trust: www.dogduckandcat.co.uk/ ✓ Family Lives: www.familylives.org.uk/advice/primary/health-and-development/keeping-your-child-safe/ ✓ NSPCC: www.nspcc.org.uk/keeping-children-safe/ ✓ NSPCC PANTS rule: www.nspcc.org.uk/keeping-children-safe/support-for-parents/underwear-rule/ ✓ Protective Behaviours: www.protectivebehaviours.org/ ✓ Thinkuknow online safety: www.thinkuknow.co.uk/4_7/

WHO/WHAT/WHERE	DESCRIPTION
Scaffolding	In education, scaffolding refers to a variety of instructional techniques used to move students progressively toward stronger understanding, and ultimately greater independence, in the learning process. The term itself offers the relevant descriptive metaphor: teachers or other supporters provide successive levels of temporary support that help students reach higher levels of comprehension and skill acquisition that they would not be able to achieve without assistance. Like physical scaffolding, the supportive strategies are incrementally removed when they are no longer needed, and the teacher gradually shifts more responsibility over the learning process to the student.
School nurse	Parents and schools in the UK have access to a school nurse team. They take over from the health visiting team as the child moves to school, offering advice and support on a range of topics – such as sleep problems, constipation and toileting – as well as delivering the school vaccination programmes.
School years in England	School years in the UK run from 1 September each year. Statutory school age is 5–16 (pupils are strongly encouraged to stay in education to 18). Most children start school at 4 and are deemed to be 'rising 5s'. Infants and Juniors are primary school pupils. Secondary begins at Year 7 in most authorities. Prior to statutory school age, children may attend preschool, nursery or *Foundation Stage* between ages 2 and 4. *Infants – Key Stage 1* (Reception pupils will be 5 during the academic year; Year 1 pupils will be 6; Year 2 pupils will be 7) *Juniors – Key Stage 2* (Year 3 pupils will be 8 during the academic year; Year 4 pupils will be 9; Year 5 pupils will be 10; Year 6 pupils will be 11)
Sense	Sense provides support and information as well as activities and respite for everyone living with complex disabilities or who is deafblind. www.sense.org.uk/
Sensory avoidance	Some children are oral defensive. They may hate certain textures and have trouble with solid food. Some children do not like to be touched, and other children will avoid touching certain textures. This used to be called tactile defensiveness, but it is recognised as a much wider issue now and is termed sensory avoidance.

WHO/WHAT/WHERE	DESCRIPTION
	Some children hate loud noise or become overwhelmed if there are too many different noises. Ear defenders may help, but children with sight impairment need to use their hearing as much as possible. Other children will not go into a bathroom that has a hand-drier. You may find school has to turn them off (because your child cannot predict when they will come on). The child may need a sensory assessment from an occupational therapist (see above), who may recommend a sensory diet (see below).
Sensory diet	A range of activities planned by an occupational therapist (see above) to help a child with sensory issues feel more comfortable, or be alert or calm, at the correct times. It can form part of a sensory integration programme.
Sensory integration	Jean Ayres defined sensory integration as *'The neurological process that organises sensation from one's own body and from the environment and makes it possible to use the body effectively with the environment.'* Effectively, this means that the brain organises all the different sensory inputs to make sense of everything and enable to body to do what it needs to do. There are many more senses than most people realise. However, usually vision is the one that ties all the inputs together, so children with severe vision impairments may be at a significant disadvantage when integrating the senses. www.sensoryintegration.org.uk/
Sensory seeking	Some children enjoy and seek out particular sensations. Oral sensory seekers will put everything in their mouths. Some children love the sound and vibration from a hand-drier or hair-drier. Occasionally they may forget to return from the bathroom, because they have become fascinated by the noise of the drier. Other children need physical pressure or weight to be comfortable. They may like to squeeze up close or request hugs. The child may need a sensory assessment from an occupational therapist (see above), who may recommend a sensory diet (see above).
Separation anxiety	All children develop separation anxiety, usually sometime between 6 months and 3 years. It is a normal part of development and usually disappears without intervention. It is only a problem if it causes extreme distress or persists beyond normal developmental stages. Speak to your health visitor (see above) or school nurse (see above) in the first instance.

WHO/WHAT/WHERE	DESCRIPTION
Severe sight impairment	The term used on the formal CVI (Certificate of Vision Impairment) registration document as an alternative to 'blind'. 'Blind' implies no vision at all, which is only rarely the case.
Sight impaired	This replaces 'partially sighted' on the registration document (see severe sight impairment above).
Sleep	Sleep can be a problem for many children, but particularly those with certain conditions or a poor understanding of time. The following organisations all provide support: https://sleepcouncil.org.uk/ https://sleepcouncil.org.uk/sleep-advice-scenarios/meet-daisy-sleep-advice-for-children/ Cerebra also provides specialist advice and support on sleep: https://cerebra.org.uk/download/sleep-a-guide-for-parents/ Your health visitor or school nurse (see entries above) will also be able to advise on sleep.
Special school	Special schools offer specialist provision to meet particular needs. They have small classes and specialist staff. www.goodschoolsguide.co.uk/special-educational-needs/schools/special-schools
Speech and language therapist (SALT)	Speech and language therapists provide life-changing treatment, support and care for children and adults who have difficulties with communication, or with eating, drinking and swallowing.
Tactile learner	Tactile learners learn primarily through touch or verbal input, and have no access to print and very limited visual images. They will probably use Braille or need access to speech on computers.
Transition	Transition is the process of moving from one state or setting to another – for instance, moving from home to school, or from primary to secondary school. It is a time of change that can have a great deal of impact on a child.
Tummy time	Tummy time is the time a baby spends on their tummy during the day. It helps baby develop neck, back and shoulder muscles (which are necessary to meet developmental milestones). For more information on tummy time, see Pathways.org: https://pathways.org/topics-of-development/tummy-time/
Verbal directions	Explain what you are doing clearly and concisely using language familiar to the child. New terminology should be explained in context. Allow the child time to process what is being said or ask questions to ensure understanding.

WHO/WHAT/WHERE	DESCRIPTION
Vestibular system	The vestibular system is one of the body's senses. It is located in the inner ear and is the main contributor to the sense of balance and spatial orientation . It tells the body where it is in space and which way up it is, in order to coordinate movement and balance. The brain uses information from the vestibular system (along with proprioception) to calculate exact force and movement. Vestibular system dysfunction can cause vertigo and motion sickness.
VICTA Parent Portal	This is a one-stop information hub for all parents and carers raising a child who is blind or partially sighted. It has a wealth of information covering topics from early years to assistive technology, and directs readers to many other organisations who can help. www.victa.org.uk/introducing-victa-parent-portal/
Wikki Stix®	Reusable flexible waxed strands that can be moulded into shapes or pressed onto a page to produce raised pictures. Wikki Stix® offer constructive and imaginative play. They are safe, non-toxic and durable. www.youtube.com/watch?v=1Fi5OxMs1yo
WonderBaby	*WonderBaby*.org is dedicated to helping parents of young children with visual impairments as well as children with multiple disabilities. The website has sections on toys and recreation, growth and development, Braille and literacy, sensory activities, iPads and apps, and orientation and mobility: www.wonderbaby.org/
Words for Life	Words for Life is the National Literacy Trust's website for parents. It has an amazing collection of songs and rhymes to use with your child (www.wordsforlife.org.uk/songs). Visit the main website for literacy news, support for schools and more information about their work: www.wordsforlife.org.uk/ The National Literacy Trust also has another project, Small Talk (https://small-talk.org.uk/), run with the Department for Education. It aims to help parents to chat, play and read with their child at home as much as possible.
World Health Organization (WHO)	WHO works worldwide to promote health, keep the world safe, and serve the vulnerable. www.who.int/

Further reading

CHILD DEVELOPMENT

Blythe, Sally Goddard (2005) *The Well Balanced Child: Movement and Early Learning,* 2nd edition. Stroud: Hawthorn Press.

A manifesto for a 'whole body' approach to learning which integrates the brain, senses, movement and play. Includes details on reflexes and the effects if they are retained.

Meggitt, Carolyn (2012) *Child Development, An Illustrated Guide,* 3rd edition [with DVD]. Harlow: Pearson Education.

Includes basic information on theories of child development. 2nd edition covers birth to 16 years.

Pound, Linda (2008) *How Children Learn: From Montessori to Vygotsky – Educational Theories and Approaches.* London: Step Forward Publishing.

Theories of development and learning in a straightforward format.

Sharma, Ajay and Cockerill, Helen (2014) *Mary Sheridan's From Birth to Five Years: Children's Developmental Progress,* 4th edition. Abingdon: Routledge.

An updated guide to development in the first five years of life, based on Mary Sheridan's seminal work. For health, education and social care professionals, or anyone concerned with the developmental progress of preschool children.

EYES AND VISION

Bowman, Richard, Bowman, Ruth and Dutton, Gordon (2010) *Disorders of Vision in Children* [CD-ROM]. London: RNIB. First published in print by RNIB in 2001.

www.ssc.education.ed.ac.uk/resources/vi&multi/eyeconds/list.html

A detailed list of eye conditions from the Scottish Sensory Centre.

FOUNDATION ILS

Newman, Sarah (2004) *Stepping Out: Using Games and Activities to Help Your Child with Special Needs.* London: Jessica Kingsley.

Newman, Sarah (2008) *Small Steps Forward: Using Games and Activities to Help Your Pre-School Child with Special Needs,* 2nd edition. London: Jessica Kingsley.

Sarah Newman provides a range of simple practical ideas together with an explanation of how these might help the child – all written from her own perspective as a parent of a child with special needs.

INCLUSION IN EARLY YEARS

RNIB (2001) *Focus on Foundation: Including Children who are Blind or Partially Sighted in Early Years Settings.* London: RNIB. www.rnib.org.uk/sites/default/files/focus_on_foundation_0.pdf

Offers an explanation of foundation stage and early years at school and promotes inclusion of pupils with vision impairment.

PLAY

RNIB (1995) *Play it My Way: Learning Through Play with Your Visually Impaired Child.* London: HMSO Publications.

RNIB (2006) *Let's Play! Toys and Play Ideas for Young Children with Vision Impairment.* www.rnib.org.uk/sites/default/files/RNIB%20Play%20Guide.pdf

Bibliography

Blythe, Sally Goddard (2005) *The Well Balanced Child: Movement and Early Learning*, 2nd edition. Stroud: Hawthorn Press.

Bowman, Richard, Bowman, Ruth and Dutton, Gordon (2010) *Disorders of Vision in Children* [CD-ROM]. London: RNIB. First published in print by RNIB in 2001.

Gallahue, David L. and Ozmun, John C. (2006) *Understanding Motor Development: Infants, Children, Adolescents Adults*, 6th edition. London: McGraw-Hill.

McLinden, Mike (2002) *Learning Through Touch: Supporting Children with Visual Impairment and Additional Difficulties*. Abingdon: David Fulton.

Mason, Heather and McCall, Stephen (eds) (1997) *Visual Impairment: Access to Education for Children and Young People.* Abingdon: David Fulton.

Meggitt, Carolyn (2012) *Child Development, An Illustrated Guide*, 3rd edition [with DVD]. Harlow: Pearson Education.

Newman, Sarah (2008) *Small Steps Forward: Using Games and Activities to Help Your Pre-School Child with Special Needs*, 2nd edition. London: Jessica Kingsley.

Norris, M., Spaulding, P. J. and Brodie, F. H. (1957) *Blindness in Children.* Chicago, IL: University of Chicago Press.

Pogrund, R. L., Lambert, J. and Fazzi, D. L. (eds) (1992) *Early Focus: Working with Young Blind and Visually Impaired Children and Their Families.* New York: American Foundation for the Blind Press.

Jerry Webster (2019) 'Chaining Forward and Chaining Backwards.' *ThoughtCo*, 30 January. www.thoughtco.com/chaining-forward-and-chaining-backwards-3110581

WEBSITES

Department for Education/Department of Health (2015) *Special Educational Needs and Disability Code of Practice: 0 to 25 Years*, January. London: DfE/DoH. https://assets.publishing.service.gov.uk/government/uploads/system/uploads/attachment_data/file/398815/SEND_Code_of_Practice_January_2015.pdf

Statutory guidance for organisations which work with and support children and young people who have special educational needs or disabilities.

https://pathways.org/all-ages/brochures/

Brochures for reference or sharing.

www.sensoryintegration.org.uk/

Accredited, high-quality sensory integration courses.

World Health Organization (2019) *Guidelines on Physical Activity Sedentary Behaviour and Sleep Age Under 5 Years of Age*. World Health Organization. https://apps.who.int/iris/handle/10665/311664. License: CC BY-NC-SA 3.0 IGO

https://apps.who.int/iris/bitstream/handle/10665/311664/9789241550536-eng.pdf?sequence=1&isAllowed=y

OTHER ONLINE RESOURCES

Information About Vision Impairment: Guide for Parents. London: RNIB. www.rnib.org.uk/sites/default/files/APDF-ENG021603_Early%20Support%20Parents%20Information.pdf

Let's Play: Toys and Play Ideas for Young Children with Vision Impairment. London: RNIB. www.rnib.org.uk/sites/default/files/APDF-RE190111%20Let%27s%20Play%202019-v06.pdf

Messy and Muddy: A Guide to Outdoor Play for Children with Vision Impairment. London: RNIB. www.rnib.org.uk/sites/default/files/APDF-RE181123_Messy%20and%20Muddy.pdf

Parties and Playdates – Including a Child with Vision Impairment in Social Activities. London: RNIB. www.rnib.org.uk/parties-and-playdates-including-child-vision-impairment-social-activities

Teaching and Learning Guidance. London: RNIB. www.rnib.org.uk/health-social-and-education-professionals/education-professionals/teaching-and-learning-guidance